Exposing the Ps

Exposing the Psalms

Unmasking their beauty, art, and power for a new generation

Peter Nevland

Authentic

20 19 18 17 16 15 14   7 6 5 4 3 2 1

First published 2014 by Authentic Media Limited
52 Presley Way, Crownhill, Milton Keynes, MK8 0ES.
www.authenticmedia.co.uk

British Library Cataloguing in Publication Data

A catalogue record for this book is available from the British Library

ISBN 978-1-86024-903-7
978-1-78078-237-9 (e-book)

Cover Design by Resound Media Ltd www.resoundmedia.co.uk
Printed and bound by CPI Group (UK) Ltd., Croydon, CR0 4YY

For all who dare to dream and do . . .
You have no idea how big God dreams and does for
you.

Contents

Contents

Contents

Lost in Time

Say the word "Paris," and the Eiffel tower, cafés, the Louvre, French food, romance, maybe female armpit hair springs to mind. Use the phrase "shake it like a Polaroid" – like Outkast did in their 2003 hit song, "Hey Ya!" – and you can picture a Polaroid print drying in someone's hand. Of course, you probably know they're really talking about gyrating booties on the dance floor, not Polaroid pictures. How long will it take for a new generation to have no idea what that phrase means? Kids today have never experienced an instant "Polaroid" with a white border from a cheap camera. In a hundred years who will remember Outkast? What about a thousand years, or four?

When you read the name "Tyre," what comes to mind? I'll bet you feel and see nothing . . . unless you grew up in Israel or Lebanon. If you're like me you have no idea what it means for God to make your horn grow. And yet the phrase can be found in Psalm 18, 75, 89, 92, 98, 112, 132, and 148. Do you have a horn? Is it growing? Can you tell me how to get one? We're familiar with the psalms, but everyone in today's Western culture misses so much of the deeper story.

The writers of the psalms didn't just throw out city names or phrases at random. These are the most brilliant songs and poems encompassing 5,000 years of Hebrew culture. Plus, most of the authors (there are a bunch of writers represented in the psalms in addition to David) were trained songwriters and poets. They chose instantly recognizable words to their audience; symbols to awaken memories, emotions, imagery both shocking and provoking.

To explain each one would have resulted in easily forgotten textbooks. It'd be like singing songs about Newtonian physics. Cool to a few of us nerds (like me) but boring to the rest of society. That's probably why academic theology books sell in the single digits while Lady Gaga, Justin Bieber, and Gangnam Style rake in millions and millions of dollars and even more YouTube views. You can find thick books that three people have read dedicated to which Bible translation is the most accurate, or whether the psalms were written pre-Davidic, neo-Davidic, post-exilic, or . . . yawn.

Meant to Be Experienced

You have to experience the psalms to understand them. They're art, not essays. You understand art when it surrounds and barrages your senses, like it would at a gallery, a museum, or in an artist's studio surrounded by paint and canvases. This book is a gallery where you can play with the art. Step out of your world and into theirs. Engage the imagination God gave you. Do it now. Switch on!

Hebrew worship always spoke or sang the psalms out loud. Most of the time the words were accompanied by orchestras of stringed and percussive instruments. The Hebrews indulged in words and music to arouse the imagination, just like poets and songwriters do today. But they didn't rhyme sounds as much as Western poetry does. Instead they used repetitive lines or phrases to emphasize meaning or signal complete changes in tone or subject. Themes became apparent as they spoke or sang out stanzas that paralleled or contrasted with each other.

Not only did the Hebrews' symbols and writing style differ, they viewed the world from an alternate perspective. We tend to think that time, technology, and knowledge make us smarter than they were. But is that really true, or have we forgotten as much as we've learned? Or do we simply do things differently?

Let's find out shall we? Answer these questions quickly. Write down your answers if you want to:

What do you use to clean your teeth?

Where do you go to get water?

How long does a good wedding last?

What do you take for an upset stomach?

Pretty easy, right? Now what if you didn't have a toothbrush or toothpaste? How would you clean your teeth?

Where would you get running water if you didn't have a faucet in your house? How much would you get and where would you store it?

How come your wedding celebrations are so short? Why don't they last a week or more? Do you not care about marriage?

What if no pharmacy existed? Which plant or herb would calm your stomach?

An ancient child could answer these simple questions but very few of us have any idea what we would do without our modern conveniences. You probably didn't even realize how biased you and I both are. That's okay. Fish don't realize they're swimming in water either.

You miss so much richness in the psalms, because you live in the twenty-first century and didn't grow up in Israel. You miss even more reading them silently or line-by-line. They're not an exercise for your intellect alone. Their power comes when they touch your emotions. When they scream with anguish in your forehead, bask your skin in grassy velvet, wrap your heart in the security of oppression's death, or giggle your face with joy.

I want to expose you to a fresh look at ancient words and ideas long covered by oceans of time. Get your favorite Bible version and follow along. (I promise I won't use words like "hermeneutics" and "exegesis.") Clean away centuries of dust and culture to discover the beauty, the life, the power that the original writers intended. You'll see the best Hebrew songs and poetry emerge from the waves, powerful and radiant again. You might even glimpse a new viewpoint of the God who inspired them in the first place.

My Approach

I'm just as lost when it comes to ancient imagery as you are. Despite being a writer myself, I'm sitting in front of my computer waiting for my car to get fixed in Fort Worth, Texas. That's a bit of time and distance between 700BC Jerusalem. I have no illusions of thinking that I know the full extent of their meaning or who God is. I'm not hoping to end the discussion of what each psalm means. That would require a much bigger book and way more brainpower than my skull contains. I've only written the first sentence in a new chapter.

Here are the steps I used to analyze each psalm. Don't be content to read this book and either agree or disagree. Get out a Bible. Take notes. Write out your thoughts. Feel free to challenge what I've discovered. Talk about it with a friend or a group of people. You'll learn and remember so much more. Okay, sermon over. On to the steps:

1. Ask God to show you what He wants you to see.
2. Read one psalm.
3. Think about that psalm.
4. Look for repeating patterns (for example, three sections of seven verses, repeated phrases, or where the *Selah*'s break it up).
5. Check out different Bible translations and see what each adds to your understanding. Each translation has its own strengths and weaknesses, so utilize a variety (what a gift that we have so many!). Dig even deeper into the possible Hebrew meanings in different concordances and commentaries.
6. Research the history surrounding whatever place names, people, and objects that particular psalm contains.
7. Consider the character of God as revealed in the rest of the Bible and your own experience.
8. Ask wise leaders about anything that doesn't make sense to you.
9. Write your own story, song, poem, or create some other kind of art (could actually fit anywhere from steps 4–9).

The result of me following these steps is the book you have in front of you. Rather than explaining every detail (makes me sleepy just thinking about it), I tried to understand each psalm and then write a story (either modern or ancient) that plunges you into the feelings and surroundings of each psalm. Occasionally I've pointed out essential symbolism or important elements of structure that get missed in most Bible translations.

Sometimes I've researched the Hebrew and attempted to write my own paraphrase of the psalm so you get a clearer understanding. Occasionally, you'll see that I've split lines or phrases in other places than verses have divided them in your Bible. I just used my poet's/writer's intuition and did that where it made more sense, kind of like the original translators did when they decided to divide the Bible into chapters and verses for easy reference. But then it's back into the experience . . .

Let your heart race as David escapes enemy clutches. Thrill as you dance and shout at the biggest celebration you can imagine. Smell the burning flesh and slip on the blood involved in sacrifice. Feel your anger explode at injustice. Melt in the tenderness of God's love.

Once the story finishes for each chapter, I've written some open-ended follow-up questions. If you're going through this book on your own, write out your answers. If you're in a group, split into smaller groups so that everyone gets a chance to respond with more than a sentence for each question. Don't settle for easy, correct-sounding answers. Open up your feelings. Be vulnerable. Listen to each other. Listen to what God says in response.

Finally, I've written a poem or song with each chapter. Imagine the music and rhythms that would go with each of them. Notice how hard that is (just like reading the psalms)? Eventually, you'll be able to buy a digital version of text, illustrations, music, video, and cultural resources that lets you dive as deeply into the psalms as you'd like. But until that dream comes to life, you'll have to use the words on these pages as the spark to your petrol-soaked bonfire of imagination.

The best case scenario from this book would be millions of people engaging with the psalms, forming them into their own prayer and praise requests and then filling their communities with beauty. We don't want to rewrite the Bible. We just want to know the God that it talks about even more. And you can't do that only by thinking about Him. You have to try out what He says. He's really creative and helpful. Ask Him if you need help. Don't be afraid to follow the inspiration that whispers, "you could do this." You'll never be quite prepared. It starts with the first step. Ready?

Take a peek at the psalms' true beauty . . .

The Answer to Fear – Psalm 31

I lay sleeping the other night. A dream entered my mind. Witches scrawled their threats in blood. I awakened to two cats facing my bedroom window wailing in perfect discordant harmony. Vicki, my wife, awoke with me. Instantly we prayed.

Words stumbled out weakly as shivers raced up our spines and hair stood on end. But the more we prayed, the more our confidence grew. After some time we walked outside together and chased off the cats. Then we prayed more inside, our anger rising at the enemy's attempt at intimidation. We sensed God's power filling us and began taking back spiritual ground. Joy flooded our souls. We sang and danced, rejoicing in God's victory over whatever spiritual attack had woken us up.

Finally we got back in bed, held each other close, and prayed until peace swooshed over our souls. As I lay in bed holding Vicki, I heard the joyous chirping of a cardinal. I went to sleep and slept like a baby in God's arms for the rest of the night.

Love tends to do that to fear. Its effectiveness depends on how close a relationship you have with the One who loves. The writer of Psalm 31 knew this as well. Despite the predominant view of God from cultures surrounding him, as well as the Law of Moses, he ran right past the barriers keeping people out of God's presence and snuggled in His lap.

Put yourself in the writer's shoes. Imagine telling God your own problems, the intimidation of your enemies, your deepest feelings.

Harps lilt through the room as you speak or sing out loud (do it now; actually speak or sing this out loud) . . .

In You, Yahweh, I seek protection,
Don't let me be put to everlasting shame,

In Your justice, help me escape.
Stretch out Your ear to me.

Get me out quickly. Be my strong tower, the fortress that saves me.
I've chosen You as my hideout and fortress. For the sake of Your reputation deliver me.

Get me out of the net they hid to trap me, because You're my protection
I'm entrusting my spirit completely to Your care.

You've paid my ransom, Yahweh, the faithful God.
I turn away from those who hold onto worthless delusion, but I trust in Yahweh.

I'll spin and beam gladness, because You've seen my misery, felt the anguish of my soul and You haven't imprisoned me in my enemy's hands.

Ahhh . . . The heaviness lifts ever so slightly. Hope whispers to your feet the dream of skipping and dancing. You feel yourself beginning to trust. God's come through time and again. He protects your reputation and the tender heart that's inside. The harp returns to its original song, this time in a minor key, growing more desperate as you plead with God (do it out loud again) to free you from everlasting shame . . .

You've made room for my feet to stand.
Give your tender favor to me, Yahweh, 'cause I'm in a tight spot.

My eyes, my spirit, my emotions fail from frustration, because my life concludes in anguish and my years with groaning.
My vigor stumbles into depravity, and my bones fail.

It's not just my enemies whispering about me, it's my friends.
People I know dread my approach. People in the street avoid me.

I'm forgotten and worth less than the dead.
I'm a lost household jar.

I hear so many whispers. Fear surrounds me.
They plot against me, scheming to take my life.

But I put my trust in You, Yahweh.
I declare that "You're my God."

You hold my life in Your hands.
Pull me out of the hands of my enemies and attackers.

Let Your face light up this servant.
Save me with Your love and goodness.

Yahweh, You can't let me suffer disgrace, 'cause I call to You.
Let the guilty be disgraced and silent in the grave.

Hush all lying lips that assault the just with blatant evil.

Perhaps you're now thinking: "Yes! I'm tired of oppression, God. Bring justice and keep evil from ever oppressing again!" You're not sure about God judging you for your own actions, but you definitely want Him to protect you from obvious evil. You're taking a risk, trusting yourself to an impartial judge. Doesn't it make you see your own flaws? You yourself deserve punishment for the wrong you've committed. The only thing that saves you from immediate and eternal punishment for the slightest wrong is a greater law, one that's illogical. God can't seem to defend His heart from the love He feels when you run to His arms. And that's where you end up . . .

How vast is the treasure You've prepared for those who honor You,
What you do for those who flee to You when all can see.

The secrets of Your presence protect them from the schemes of men.
You protect them as Your treasure from contentious tongues.

Yahweh deserves all praise for His tender miracles when I was besieged.
I assumed that my end had come, but You answered my cries to You.

Love the Great I AM, all you faithful-hearted ones.
Yahweh guards those faithful to Him and fully repays the self-righteous.

Stand strong, and He'll be your steadfast heart when you fix your hope on Yahweh.

The harp finishes with a flourish. You don't just feel relief and peace; you feel strength surging through your heart. Notice what happened when you ran to God for help, exposed your fear, and surrounded yourself with truth and the security of God's peace? Fear and worry have fled the room.

The secrets of God's love surround you when you wait on Him. His mercy longs for you to run close. His arms yearn to banish the demons that have planned your demise. Snuggle up close to His heart. Knowledge can't save you. God's presence is the answer for every threat written to scare you out of sleep.

When you see the word "Yahweh"

It's important to have a good mental picture for the meaning of the name "Yahweh," since it's used constantly through the psalms. It comes from "Jah," a word for "God," and "weh," from the verb "to be." Some have suggested that this means, "The God who exists." Others have pointed out that it includes, "The God who creates." Still others have said that it means "I am who I am, you can take it or leave it." You can read tons of books about the word and spend years discussing its meaning.

Names to ancient peoples weren't just a way to distinguish one person from another. They carried the purpose and mission of someone's life. They carried with them the character traits of each individual. In fact, the first speaking of someone's name was thought to cause that person to leave the spiritual world and enter the physical world. Slightly more important than how we view it today!

Whenever a deity's name was mentioned, often a list of characteristics or attributes was attached to it. These either indicated the powers a god possessed or the mission he or she was on in the story being told. Hebrew writers used this same style to talk about God in the Bible. They often mentioned His name as "Yahweh Righteousness" or "Yahweh Provider" or "Yahweh Banner." You'll see this when you start digging through a concordance to find each instance the psalms mention "the Lord." When you do, take it as a clue to indicate which characteristic, or power, of God the psalmist wants to illustrate.

Personally, I prefer the idea that when God first told Moses His name in Exodus 3:16, He was telling him how He was going to act on Israel's behalf. He was *the God who causes to be and initiates relationship.* Every time they would have heard this particular name, it would have reminded them of the God who had formed them into a nation and entered into an eternal covenant to treat them as His favorite children.

Hebrew tradition eventually attached such high reverence to Yahweh being correctly pronounced that they wouldn't say the word aloud. Sometimes I wonder if this defeated the whole purpose of the name – to remind them of God's desire to be continually close and intimate with the nation and people He created. It's good to be right. But I get the feeling that God will keep you as correct as you need to be if you just focus on staying as close to Him as possible.

Follow-up questions

1. What fear came to your mind while reading this chapter?
2. How do you normally choose to react?
3. What will you do the next time it tries to scare you?

Fleeing to Rest

I'm fleeing to rest in Your safety.
I've hidden myself in Your strength.
Don't let me go down in disgrace, O God,
You can't help but do right,
Pull me out.
Look my way.
Hear my plea.
Be the fortress that shelters this frail heart.
Who You are,
The immovable mountain,
Unconquerable fortress,
Tower that no one could scale.
It's why Your love illumines,
Your whispers urge,
Your power breaks every trap.
Every last drop of my soul rests wholly in Your care,
Faithful God who pays the debt I owe.
I turn my back on lies and woe
I rest in the God who lives,

My hands clap shackles free,
Feet skip liberty,
Mountains bow down to mercy.

Because You saw my pain,
Added Your tears,
Stayed until the sunlight dried my cheeks.
Weakness lost in harbors of care,
These feet smile safely, far from fear.
Turn your tenderness to me now or I will fail.
Everything's screaming pain,
Stabbing through heart and thought,

Trains of grief stretching years,
A trail of groans and past mistakes.
My shame corrodes. Depression steals the sun away.
If eyes hurled hate from enemies, I could stand,
But friends have shut me out, run in fear.
Silence answers.
No one hears my brokenness.
Lies and then fear
Lies and fear,
Fear and then lies
They rise with lies and fear,
"Let's plunge his soul to hell!"

My hands clap shackles free,
Feet skip liberty,
Mountains bow down to mercy.

But I fled to rest in Your safety,
Staked trembling hope in the strength of who You are,
Through summer, winter, drought, and flood,
Save my soul like sweet rain.
Part their armies with love
Beaming from Your face,
Kindness warming the night with peace.
Don't let me drown in disgrace, O King,
My voice calls only for You.
May evil men find their doom,
Forever locked in barren lands,
Unable to coil their crafty plans
May the righteous forever stand untouched by regret.
No conceited looks or forked tongue words
Can reach them with Your face in view.
I declared my own disaster way too soon,
But You heard,

Cracked the skies,
Split the fortress walls of pride to rescue me.

My hands clap shackles free,
Feet skip liberty,
Mountains bow down to mercy.

You rescued me.
Little, weak, and helpless me.
Let Him see your hearts, you faithful ones,
Pour out your thankful songs.
The arrogant get what they deserve.
His voice soothes frightened, frazzled nerves.
The God who lives has pledged His word
To anchor every hope that rests in Him.

Are You Happy Enough?
– Psalm 100

"You're not happy enough."

"What? I thought I was . . ."

"Ya can't come in."

"But why? I *feel* good. I *feel* happy."

"How would anyone know? If you were happy, you'd be smilin', skippin', singin'. You might laugh, maybe put your hands in the air. You might kneel with a smile on your face or shout out how good God is. But you're not doing any of those. You're . . . Not . . . Happy."

"So I can't just be happy on the inside?"

"Look, buddy. What's your problem? You wanna make trouble?"

"No, I just want to . . ."

The guard leans in close. "There's a party goin' on in there. I start lettin' people in that don't know how to celebrate, pretty soon no one's smilin', no one's dancin', no silly games or overloadin' on pleasure . . ."

"Overload on pleasure? Inside?"

"As much pleasure as ya want. Your tongue erupting in sweet sugary bursts. Smells your nose would kill for, and the music . . ."

"The music?"

"I hear, if ya don't watch it, the music will make ya feel like you're in another world. Parts might start getting active that ya didn't plan on getting active, if ya know what I mean." He starts chuckling. This guy's a weirdo.

"C'mon, ya gotta let me in."

"Nope."

"Just this once."

"Not a chance."

"I said . . . !"

Four strong hands clamp you from behind and lift you off the ground. You're not in control anymore, and you're traveling in the opposite direction of the gate. You pick up speed. The hands clamp tighter. They release . . . for a moment you're soaring . . . and then your face eats dirt.

If you felt good before, you don't now. Everyone walking by you on the road offers compassionate looks. Some rush over to help you, but you shrug them off. You wipe the mud off your cheek, crack your neck, and tramp back home. You spend the day alone while everyone else parties. This miserable day's gonna last forever.

❊   ❊   ❊

So, what if that was the requirement for entering a church? You can't just *feel* fine. You have to show by some outward action that you're happy. If that requirement produced the kind of party I described, everyone would want to be there. It wouldn't matter if you agreed with the sermons or not. You'd want to experience something better than anything you'd tried before. Too bad you can't force people to be happy, except in Israel.

In Israel, they had planned national parties (still do). Five times a year they were commanded by God to celebrate, to feast, to party, to be happy. The whole nation traveled to celebrate at one spot, or at least, they were supposed to. People brought thanksgiving offerings of animals, crops, oil, and wine. They danced. They played music. They sang songs. Psalm 100 is one of them. You're about to experience it. It's not quiet.

Before you look at the psalm itself, I have to explain some things, or you won't have as cool an experience. You've probably heard that there are seven Hebrew words for "praise" used in the Old Testament. If you haven't, there are. I've left them in my paraphrase of the verses so you can see which ones are where, since English translations of the Bible sometimes make them hard to spot. Here are four of the seven, which you'll need for this psalm:

Yadah – a verb with a root, meaning "the extended hand, to throw out the hand, therefore to worship with extended hand." According to the lexicon, the opposite meaning is "to bemoan, the wringing of the hands."

Towdah – from the same principle root word as *yadah*, but it is used more specifically. It literally means "an extension of the hand in adoration, avowal, or acceptance." It's used for thanking God for "things not yet received" as well as things already at hand. So every time you see the word *towdah*, picture yourself throwing your hands up to God in thanks. Feel free to try out how it feels and actually do it.

Tehillah – derived from the word *halal* meaning "the singing of *halals*, to sing or to laud; perceived to involve music, especially singing; songs of the Spirit." I'll talk about the word *halal* a little later, but for now think of it as a combination of shining and celebrating loudly. *Tehillah* was often used when a group of people would sing, inspired by the Holy Spirit, all at once.

Barak – means "to kneel down, to bless God as an act of adoration."

Okay, Hebrew dictionary lesson over. Strike up the band. Tickle the drums with an uptempo beat. Everyone's feelin' it. You gotta move your feet. You gotta dance and sing. Horns blow, flutes whistle, strings stroke the air. It's a National . . . Celebration . . . par-teeeee! They stop.

One guy shouts at the top of his lungs . . .

Shout victoriously to Yahweh, all the earth!
Serve Yahweh with joy!
Enter His presence with triumphant shouts.

Everyone around you yells at the top of their lungs. The ground under your feet trembles as the drums march on. Pretty soon the singers sing out in unison. Almost everyone around you knows the song and sings along. The whole nation is singing together . . .

> Experience that Yahweh alone is God.
> He fashioned us, we didn't.
> We're His people, the flock He shepherds.

A girl grabs your hand, and you're dancing. You grab a little boy as you run past him. Now you're in a circle. The drums lead all the instruments. Circles of dancers are everywhere. Now the music returns to the very beginning melody . . .

> Enter His gates with *towdahs*.
> And His courts with *tehillahs*
> *Yadah* to Him and *barak* His name.

Everyone throws up their hands and tells God what they're thankful for. "You made my father a respected man at the gate this year. Thank you, Yahweh!" you yell. People bow. They sing, smiling and crying all at once. The music builds until everyone shouts in unison . . .

> For Yahweh is good!
> His kindness is forever!
> His faithfulness to all generations!

When it's finally time to take Baruch, your best sheep, to offer to God, you're pretty sure you've sung that song thirty-seven times. Four sets of triplets. The first two reflect the last two. Compare the second triplet to the third triplet. It's not just saying that Yahweh is the only King of everything. It's telling you that He's a good King. He made you, and gives you His love and kindness forever. You're part of the flock He personally watches and takes care of forever, just like you've cared for Baruch.

"Yahweh's worth it," you say as you hand the leash to the priest. He smiles and takes the reins, hands covered in blood. "I wonder if he likes his job?" you think to yourself. Then he shouts the same prayer he shouts for everyone else and slaughters Baruch. Pretty soon you're eating the tastiest roast lamb, your best dedicated to Yahweh. It never feels normal. It's hard to sacrifice your prize and eat it. But no other nation you know of has as much fun at celebrations as Israel.

※ ※ ※

Most Israelites never actually experienced that scene. Apart from David, Solomon, Hezekiah, and Josiah, none of Israel's kings celebrated those feasts. God had planned for regular, national (maybe even international) parties, but His people settled for something less. They went separately at different times of the year to give their offerings. Sometimes the priests became corrupt, keeping the best parts of the sacrifice for themselves. In Jesus' time, someone would tell you that you couldn't get in, not because you weren't happy, but because your offering wasn't holy enough. Of course *they* could provide you with a better one, for a very high price. No wonder Jesus took time to braid a whip.

Many churches behave the same way today. "Change yourself, and you can come into our church," people hear outside the "fellowship hall." "You can be pure and boring here!" our actions shout, while we follow the rules. There's nothing wrong with commitment and reverence. Our fast-food culture needs more of that than ever. But commitment and reverence without joy and ecstasy is like a marriage without intimacy: two people forced to share the same space with someone they don't know and never will. You can't have one without the other. Feel free to read about it in Revelation 3 when Jesus talks to the church in Sardis and Laodicea.

I remember visiting my grandparents' church as a seven year old. The organ played quietly and the people sang in pews. "Why's it so quiet, Mom?" I remember asking.

The church I grew up in had wild dancing, shouting, banners, kneeling, and people inspired by the Spirit of God to give messages. Just the worship by itself sometimes lasted for two and a half hours.

Maybe you don't do it that way. Cool. Worship God with all your heart, mind, and body in whatever style that draws you closest to Him. But if God's really changing your heart, it'll find its way onto your face, hands, and even your bouncing toes. Maybe that's weird to you. It was normal to me. It was alive.

The difference isn't your personality. It's how much you've experienced it. The things you and I long for aren't necessarily the best, they're just what make us most comfortable, what we're used to. Would you rather be alive and uncomfortable? Or comfy and dead?

Psalm 45 says that the King has more joy than anyone around Him. You want to be like Him, right? I sure do. Feel free to sing along . . .

> If you're happy and you know it clap your hands (clap clap).
> If you're happy and you know it clap your hands (clap clap).
> If you're happy and you know it then your life will surely show it.
> If you're happy and you know it clap your hands (clap clap).

Are *you* happy enough?

Follow-up questions

1. Think of the time that you felt the happiest in your life. What physical reaction did you make?
2. Who gets the happiest at your church?
3. Can you be happy when you're staring down problems, or a bully? Why or why not?

I Want Noise!

I want noise!
I want a song!
I want it loud!
I want a throng of drunken, revelrous madmen rejoicing and
    hootin' hollerin' happy,
Lettin' loose a shout of victory,
A celebration explosion of thanks,
A dance of goofball pranks and gaudy glee flung up to the sky.
I want to cry tears of joy and gratefulness to the ground,
That purifying sound of splashing and giggling,
Gurgling, cuddling, bubbling,
Bust out the booties and start 'em shakin' in a dance that tramples
    the endless monotony of day to day trance and sway,
'Cause I want to break out and display the eruptive firework,
    humongous, oversized, can't-be-penalized, shackle-splitting,
    eardrum-crashing, church-wall-smashing hurricane of gladness
    to the unmatched Creator of the world!

And I'm not just talkin' about the pretty, little Hans Brinker look on
    my white-boy face.
I'm calling every race and color,
Smothered with beautiful, bright, shiny, and glittery gobs of
    culture
Running together and over and under, smeared around in
    combinatorial shades.
We're gonna raid the locked-up cabinet of goodies wrapped in
    chains and shameful pictures of pain and regret,
'Cause it's time to crank up a jukebox of peace and get our stolen
    brothers and sisters released
To boogie and shake and shudder with an earthquake of
    worldwide, clean your insides out, happiness, hallelujah
    lovin'!

Don't be afraid to stop doin' what you've been doin' and start
chompin' on the taste-good, juicy fruit of an excited heart serving
its Maker.

Get in that margarita shaker and stir up those untuned vocal
strings,

'Cause I want to hear you sing,

Let some melody come skippin' out of your mouth in a childhood
game right where the eyes of God smile approvingly,

His holy butt getting joltin' jiggy with your little wiggy wag grab
bag of disco moves!

Don't lose this chance to prance this thought in your mind.

You didn't make your own behind, buttocks, gluteus flatulence, or
whatever choice, three-letter word you decide to use.

It was a gift to wear along with those wooly shoes and the rest of
your sheep-covered skin.

Is this news to your fears?

Release from the queer, quackpot notion that you've got to
conform your posterior to the rigid, right angle pews of a
stone-age way of sleeping?

Let's start the tuba leaping out a beat,

Keeping the streets lined with a raucous throng ready to enter the
King's palace with praise for the maker of the sun, stars, and rain,

Throw up our hands as the sensory overload of presents, delights,
and pleasures fills up our expanding brains,

Drink the healing champagne of His merciful, eternal name,

Because He's good, and loves you,

And the invisible, free-to-all reality of that is never going to
change.

Trust Me, You Want to Be the Underdog – Psalm 83

People love to *root* for the underdog; the girl who ascends from slave to princess; the local business that outsmarts a giant corporation; the weakling that takes down a bully. Not many of us actually want to *be* the underdog.

"Sure, put me at the bottom of a pit with monsters that are way bigger and stronger than me!" "Yeah, send me to a new school where I'm the smallest, everyone calls me names, laughs at me and I walk home with bruises and spit stains." Sounds fun! Sign me up!

I guess that's why we root for them. We all face our own monsters, and bullies. So, if you see an underdog overcoming, maybe you can as well.

Israel felt like the ultimate underdog as a nation. God had taken a million people from being slaves in Egypt to carving out a nation of their own. But almost all those nations and people groups they fought against still lived nearby. And they considered the land that Israel lived on to be their property.

Sure, God had helped Israel with miraculous victories and declared the whole land to be their possession. That didn't matter. Those people groups worshiped their own gods. They hated Israel and surrounded them on every side. They continually schemed and fought to wipe Israel off the map.

So in Psalm 83 Asaph (or his school of writers) calls on the God who he knows has the power to save his nation. "Don't sit back,

God!" "Don't let us handle it on our own." "Look, they're not just our enemies. They hate you." "They're coming out of the cracks. They're getting noisy. They're growing in strength, making plans. They're gonna attack Your people. They want to annihilate us. They don't even want anyone to remember that we existed. You gonna let that happen, God?"

God had sworn to Israel repeatedly that they would be His special people. He'd made a covenant with them and then taken the responsibility of maintaining that covenant Himself. To an ancient mind, this was almost unfathomable, the more respected party saying, "May I be ripped in two and destroyed if I ever break this oath of loyalty to you." So anyone who wanted to destroy Israel, wanted to destroy God too. They saw it as impossible to love one and hate the other.

So in verse 5 Asaph accuses all these nations of gathering together to fight against God. "It's you they want to obliterate, God!" Then he lists them. He starts with the people closest to Israel, Edom (or Esau), Jacob's brother. They called him Edom because it meant red, and he apparently had red hair. It's also a subtle way to paint the picture of blood on his hands.

Now Asaph names Ishmael, Isaac's older half-brother and rival who made fun of him. Moab, the descendants of one of Lot's daughters, conceived by incest, comes next. The Moabites tried to curse Israel on its way out of Egypt and opposed the people from that time on. The Hagrites, an offshoot of the Ishmaelites, rounds out the first four. All of these lived to the south and east of Israel and had hated them for centuries.

Now Asaph draws a circle, starting with north and west of Israel, Gebal – or Byblos (depending on which translation you're reading), birthplace of paper and capital of Phoenicia. He continues east of Israel with Ammon, another incestual descendant of Lot. Then he returns to Amalek in the south, who had picked off the weak of Israel since their flight from Egypt. Just the mention of those three would have made any Jew feel the noose draw tight around his or her neck.

Now he adds the Philistines, Israel's most current enemy who lived on the west, the Mediterranean coast, and spawned Goliath. Finally he mentions Tyre, the arrogant island city that despised Israel for its lack of wealth and riches. "Even Assyria has come from far away and joined up with them. They're all out to fight us and steal what You've given us, God."

Here comes a *Selah*, time for the instruments to set the mood, maybe change the tune. I can't imagine singing a song, complaining that everyone's against me. Oh, wait. That's grunge and emo and Taylor Swift's songs about boyfriends.

Verses 9 through 16 start delivering Israel's request for each kingdom, paralleling the first eight verses. Midian and Sisera's defeats both started with loud sounds, as if the Lord was speaking. Jabin, who perished at En Dor, boasted against Israel, tried to rule over them (lifted up their head), defied God, and was annihilated.

Oreb and Zeeb and Zebah and Zalmunna were Midianite princes that raided Israel, thinking they could take everything good from Israel for themselves. They also killed Gideon's brothers, as a way to blot out Gideon's father's name.

Compare the image of "whirling dust" and "chaff before the wind" (NKJV) to verse 5's image of an alliance. Asaph's telling God to blow 'em away in disunity.

Edom and the Ishmaelites, and Moab and the Hagrites lived either in tents or on mountains and would have feared an out of control fire that surrounded them and raged through the mountains. Gebal, Philistia, and Tyre all sat on the seacoast and would have feared ocean tempests. Ammon and Amalek get scared by God's whirlwind or "storm" since it had a dual meaning of a place east of Israel. Any far off countries (Assyria) rushing to help Israel's enemies get covered in shame.

Why? So that they will recognize that their gods are worthless and want the God that Israel knows. They've been choosing what looks good, like Lot did when he pitched his tent in the fertile fields near Sodom, instead of receiving the inheritance that God promised Abraham by faith.

So verses 17 and 18 cap it off. "Them" references all the conniving enemies that deal injustice and death to the weak and innocent. Asaph's asking God to frustrate every one of their plans and make them sick of trying. "Let the whole world laugh at their futile attempts. Let them meet divine judgment. Let them know that there's no one else but the God of Israel who has any divine influence over the earth."

Notice the lack of revenge. Unlike so many movies, Asaph doesn't want Israel's enemies to die at the end of a Jewish sword. He wants them to recognize the only true God. God's not out to annihilate people for no reason. He's protecting those who He loves and His name's reputation at the same time.

When Asaph asks God not to stay silent, he's saying, "Reveal yourself! Show how incredible You are. Don't let them oppress us anymore. The more You love and protect us, the more the world will want You."

God's the power that defeats monsters. He knows how to take down bullies. He helps underdogs and weaklings experience honor and the power that flows from His heart. It's His primary method for showing the world His power.

So, you still clenching your fist, trying to hold all the power? God can take you down. Are you hoping for revenge? Do you imagine yourself punishing those who've bullied you as badly as they've treated you? Read the last paragraph again about how God treats underdogs and bullies. I think you'd rather be the underdog.

Follow-up questions

1. Who are your enemies?
2. What usually happens when you choose what looks or feels good instead of trusting the invisible promise of God?
3. Which circumstance in your life would you most want God to change? Why?

Whatever You Do, Don't Be Silent

Whatever You do don't be silent.
Don't hide in the shadows.
Don't forget Your great strength.
Don't let Your arms hang limply.
O King of all kings, awake!

You hear their laughter,
Mocking jokes?
They've sharpened their teeth,
Planned to set me on fire,
Waiting to taunt me after math and choir.

"Let's surround him with arrows,
Poison-tipped jeers.
We'll cut out his heart,
Feed the mascot his tears.
No one will rescue.
His memory will end.
School halls will never hear his pitiful name again."

Shatter their threats.
Crush the fists they've clenched against You.
Burn the oaths they've sworn in full view.
Destroy their every plan to murder the delight of Your heart,
Humiliate and swallow me whole.

You know it's not just me.
They mock everyone different,
Crown themselves king,
Conniving and scheming,
Harassing the weak,

Stealing self-confidence,
Destroying what they could never create themselves.

Blast them in the heat of Your anger.
Bring their words back to haunt them.
Let them cower under Your rage.
Make them feel powerless.
Shake their bones with dread.
Tie them to the flagpole.
Tape a sign to their chest.
Write Your fury.
"This is what happens to those who bully the helpless.
Don't ever touch My innocent ones again."

Because it's You they've hated,
Let the whole world hear their shame.
If they swallow the destruction they've created,
Maybe then they'll desire Your name,
Your goodness,
The love you spend so freely,
The gifts You lavish on everyone who comes to You,
O God,
My Savior,
Keeper of my life.

Let everyone who opposes You
Eat empty fruit and taste unmet hope,
Lose all they own
And grope for rescue in a barren wasteland.
You're the only source of water,
The only breath of life.
Your voice spoke the universe to existence.
Don't be silent on behalf of Your child.

The Messiah, His Bride, and . . . Huh? Is This the Bible – Psalm 45

I've always struggled with Psalm 45. I get the first half of it, but then it starts getting weird in verse 10. Put yourself in my shoes as you read it.

It starts with the author's heart overflowing, his tongue being a pen, ready to write, full of a noble theme, verses for the king. Hmmm . . . he wants to write about the king and how awesome he is.

This can't just be a regular king. It's prophecy about the Savior, the Promised One who will fulfill all the world's hopes and dreams. It doesn't confuse you when he starts talking about "God blessing you forever," or "riding out victoriously," or "sinking your arrows in the heart of your enemies," because the Messiah only fights to defend people from evil and injustice. It's pure truth, humility, and justice with no corruption, unlike every human ruler the world's experienced. Cool.

You want someone to save you like that. You want someone you can trust to have perfect integrity in deciding who's right and who's wrong, who also has the power to defend the innocent and stop oppressors. Even better, His throne's going to last forever. He's always going to be good. He's always going to be the person with the most joy. Everything about Him is sweet, even down to His clothes and the people in His court. There's even going to be a queen, a bride clothed in every bit of His splendor.

You start getting excited thinking how the Messiah will be fully seen in all His glory, with His bride right there with him. It makes all those bride of Christ references in the New Testament make sense! You get to be part of His treasured friend and partner forever! It could have stopped right here, and you'd be happy. But it doesn't . . .

In verse 10 the author suddenly starts talking to this daughter, a girl or woman, telling her to forget her people and her father's house to go be with the king. Ummm . . . if He already has a bride, why does she need to leave her family to be with the King? And why, if He already has a wife, would the King desire some other girl's beauty?

It doesn't get much better when the author says to bow to Him because He's her lord, or ruler. That sets off every modern day, misogynistic warning bell in your head. And you have no idea what it means that the daughter of Tyre will bow with a gift, or that the rich will come seeking her favor. And then you lose the plot entirely . . .

What is this about how glorious the princess is in her chamber in her many-colored robes and virgin companions following behind her. Is this supposed to be some big orgy with the king? Oh, with joy and happiness they get led into His palace. For what? What the heck is going on? Are you even reading the Bible anymore?

"In place of your fathers shall be your sons"? "You will make them princes in all the earth"? "And your name will be remembered forever, by all nations"? He's talking about the girl still, right?

You figure you've missed some references. If this chapter in the Bible is one of the best Hebrew poem/songs of all time, withstanding historical scrutiny for thousands of years, it can't be about some orgy with the King, who's the Messiah. Can it?

Calm down. You're right. It's not nearly as twisted as all that. First of all, it's a song, with a musical theme to accompany it. To best understand the lyrics, you have to think like a songwriter. Songs rarely include music that continually changes all the way through. The theme gets introduced, developed, and then repeated. This song is no different. The note that goes with it says it's to the choirmaster, set to "Lilies," which is a certain song or piece of music. It further says it's a *Maskil*, which had something to do with wisdom or understanding. There are a number of psalms written as *Maskils*, and a few that are set to this specific piece of music.

The other important point to remember is that Psalm 45, like I described before, rhymes thoughts. Each section compares to or builds on the others. Consider verse 1 as something of an introduction, or possibly even a chorus. The rest divides up into two sections: the first (vv.2–9), about the King/Messiah, and the second (vv.10–17), about the girl/woman/bride. Compare the arrangement of themes for each part. You'll see that they correspond amazingly well to each other, showing masculine and feminine qualities of the same character trait.

Verses 2 and 3 talk about the King being more striking and wonderful to look at than anyone else and having grace on His lips (He's incredibly charming, with His words, not necessarily a great kisser, although He's probably that too). That's why God has poured out blessings on Him forever. "So take that power out," the psalmist says. "Put Your sword, the full amount of Your strength at Your side, ready to display Your glory and majesty. Don't hide it. Let everyone be in awe of You."

In comparison, verse 10 finds the writer imploring the girl/woman to leave her father's house and her own people to be with the King. That way, He will desire her beauty. In the place where you would expect the writer to talk about the daughter's glory and majesty, he implores her to worship the King. Her glory and majesty is found when she honors the King. She shares in His glory, blessing, majesty, honor, *and* power as she worships Him. Whoa!

The psalmist tells us the reason for the Messiah to display His power in verse 4. "Be successful because of truth, humility, and righteousness." He doesn't destroy everything and everyone who doesn't understand Him, like some human conqueror. He's guided by truth and compassion. He's only goodness, no injustice, surrounded by so much good He can't make a wrong decision. His unstoppable power (his right hand) "teaches Him awesome things." He exhales humility. He knows the perfect balance between the need to destroy evil and save those who have been deceived by it.

That Messiah will defeat all evil demonic forces and everyone who utterly sells their soul to do evil against God and His children. Even better, He'll save the ones they oppress. "His arrows are sharp . . ." He ain't playing around. He can deal with evil.

So what's the feminine counterpart to that? Verses 12 and 13 say that the "daughter of Tyre will come with a gift" and "the rich among the people will seek your favor" (NASB). To get this, you have to know what Tyre represented to the Jewish people. In 1 Kings, Tyre had the best craftsmen and building materials in the region. Hiram came from Tyre, with some other guys, to build Solomon's temple. Tyre was the capital of Phoenicia, a country known for its fleet of merchant ships throughout the world. It stood on an island, just off the coast, a sparkling jewel in the sea. The merchants could procure anything people wanted and had been exposed to everything interesting and beautiful in the ancient world. They were cultured. They were rich. They were snobby.

When Solomon went to give cities to the king of Tyre in exchange for their craftsmen making Israel beautiful, the king of Tyre said, "these are worthless!" He literally named the cities "good for nothing." Good for nothing? This wasn't Elijah in a camel hair coat he was talking to. Solomon made silver worth nothing. He had a palace and throne more luxurious than any king on earth. But still the king of Tyre turned his nose up at him! Later, in Ezekiel 28, when God proclaims judgment against Tyre, it says that the heart of its king got so proud, he thought he was a god, just like Satan did (see below for more on Solomon and the king of Tyre).

So the daughter of Tyre is that stuck-up girl in high school that's pretty, popular, and talented, and she knows it. She's Dallas in comparison to Waco; New York City to Springfield, Missouri; London to Stoke-on-Trent. She thinks she's better than you, and she'll make sure you know it. Psalm 45 says that stuck-up girl will come bowing with a gift, begging you to forget the way she treated you. She'll recognize how glorious *you've* become. Rich people will beg you to give *them* something. That's what's going to happen to your rivals. They'll never play the comparison game ever again.

27

Now the lowly girl enters the palace in verse 13. Just like the King rides clothed in power and humility in verse 4, she radiates glory within the palace. Every part of her shines with wonder, inside and out. Even the thread of her clothes sparkles with the most costly materials. No price could be too large to lavish on this girl turned royalty.

Verses 6, 7, and 8 display the full majesty of the Messiah. His kingdom, rule, and reign last forever. He's guided only by goodness and complete rightness. Evil never comes close to entering His thoughts. That's why God puts a crown on His head ("God, your God has crowned You" although the Messiah has already been declared to be "God." This is a tough concept for humans to wrap their minds around, so I'll leave it for theologians to explain God's three-in-one nature). Even better, it's a crown of joy. The Messiah bubbles with more joy than anyone around him. He's a party to be around. He's happy and genuine, and I'm in love. Even His clothes smell amazing. His palace exhales peace, richness, and complete satisfaction.

Now look at the girl-turned-princess in verses 14–16. She walks toward the King in all her beauty. It's not something weird, it's a wedding. Her sisters and friends celebrate her, dancing and singing, because they're her bridesmaids. They can't stop themselves from smiling. They enter the King's palace and give her to the King to be His queen forever. Instead of people knowing about her father and those who have gone before her, they'll remember the exploits of her children. She's going to be more famous and glorious than them all, sharing the glory right alongside the Savior.

And then each section culminates. In verse 9 we see the queen standing with the King, clothed in glory and honor. The Messiah will have a bride as beautiful as He is. A heavenly marriage will take place between God's people and their Savior. The first section shows the Messiah preparing to receive His bride. If we didn't have the second section, the picture wouldn't paint the bride's perspective.

Then verse 17 trumpets the culmination of the big day, with everybody standing before the king and queen. Remember when Prince William and Kate Middleton kissed on the balcony of Buckingham

Palace while thousands of people cheered? Psalm 45 has billions and billions of people gathered, angels, galaxies, the wealth of the entire universe, and the party lasts for the rest of time. It's the ultimate Cinderella story of rags to riches, King married to commoner, girl transformed into glory.

The creator of the Universe longs to be seen in all His glory so that He can share it with you. He wants all of humanity to partake in the intimate relationship He's experienced since before time. When your mind swells with that much hope, you'll change how you live. It'll affect every aspect of your daily life and the world around you.

Families will start spending more time together. Businesses will serve their customers better. The legal system will finally deliver justice. Evil will get banished from hearts. Children will grow up to be adults who haven't lost their innocence. Isn't that what your heart yearns for?

Unsubstantiated Solomon speculation

All of Solomon's riches were put on display and his palace built *after* he built the temple and tried to give some cities to the king of Tyre as a present. Maybe at the time when he first met him, Solomon dressed humbly, like his father. Maybe the king of Tyre's response made him feel insecure. Maybe he felt like he needed to dress and decorate and show off like the richest king in the world. Maybe it started his slow decline. I don't know. Maybe. Hmmmm.

Follow-up questions

1. What does Psalm 45's portrayal of us as His bride indicate about the value of women?
2. What can men learn about God's love from a woman's perspective?
3. What can women learn about God's love from a man's perspective?

For the King

I ready my pen,
Bridle my tongue.
My lips dance their melodies for the King,
Spilling out,
Tipping over,
Twirling tasty morsels,
Choice pearls of eager goodness.
You are fairer than all others, my Love.

Every word You utter
Drips to an open mouth,
A desperate, parched earth,
Springs of hope in a weary wasteland
Only You could be crowned with favor forever.

Stand like the King You are,
Warrior for the weak,
Conqueror of bleak death.
Plunge Your sword into snarling demons,
Sink Your arrows in enemies' hearts,
Show Your strength,
Trample their faces,
Drown them in truth,
Fill the earth with the fruit of humility,
Secrets of stars.
You last beyond the end and before the start of time.

But it's not Your power that gives You strength
Not Your greatness that wins our love.
No spot of jealousy,

No hint of pride,
Mixed motives come nowhere near to invading Your heart on the
      inside.

You turn Your back on every evil thought,
Never cause harm.
It makes Your smile genuine,
Your laugh easy.
When You enter the room,
Rest and spotlessness prance at Your side.
Your spirit sings.
The maidens dance.
At Your right hand stands the queen,
Clothed in all the honor You own.

Give me your ear, my precious one.
Trust in the counsel I speak.
Let your past sink out of reach.
The warmth of your childhood home can't compete
With your destiny laid at His feet.
Set your eyes on the King.
Fling your cares in His arms.
Let your charms stroke His face,
All His sweetness to taste

And every jealous rival,
Once proud, superior
Will bow with their gifts,
Beg for your favor,
Gaze on your beauty,
Twinkling from temples,
Woven in gold.

Your sisters dance,
Bringing you in,
Innocence flowing from dresses,
Skipping like fawns,
Filling the palace with fountains of songs.

Your children will succeed your fathers in fame.
The whole world will proclaim
Stirring tales of your deeds.
Every child will read
Of the simple girl who discovered her dreams
Desired by the Fairest of all.

We ready our pens,
Bridle our tongues.
Our lips dance their melodies for the King.

Know any Shepherds? – Psalm 23

You can't help but feel rest and peace when you read Psalm 23. The worries and cares that seemed so huge melt away in oases of vegetation. It's so easy to skip right past what it really means that Yahweh has committed Himself to being your Shepherd.

If you said "shepherd" in the days when this was written, people would have a clear picture of what a shepherd does, what he or she looks like, their tasks, challenges, attitude toward the sheep, would be able to think of friends that were shepherds. I don't have any friends who are shepherds.

Is there an equal to a shepherd in our culture? Someone who gets smelly and grubby dealing with pretty stupid animals all day and night? In ancient times, these were low class people. In today's terms, you might rank them with a night shift janitor, a manure spreader, or a fast-food server. Doesn't it seem odd that of all the occupations in the world, the most awesome Person in the universe chose the least respected job to prove His desire for a relationship with you?

He doesn't just plunge Himself into filth and shame to clean up your mistakes. His love won't let you lack any good thing. He'll lead you to safe places to rest, satisfy your thirst, and renew your spirit. Sure He's powerful. But He's humble. He's got time for you. Your needs are the most important thing on His list.

Once you've recovered from God's love assault on your brain, what does it mean for Him to lead you in paths of righteousness? You need a better word for righteousness. Posers and preachers have done a pretty good job ruining the concept. When I hear that word, my first thought is "phony" or "self-righteous." Authentic righteousness seems so hard to grasp for our modern minds.

Ancient cultures had very little concept of an inner righteousness. To them a person's actions and prosperity indicated their level of righteousness. People saw how virtuous a person was by the choices they made. In their mind rich people, kings, and priests were the most righteous of all.

The book of Job reveals a stunning departure from this mindset. Job holds to an inner righteous quality despite his suffering. While his friends say, "Just appease God's requirement for an offering. You must have done something wrong" Job refuses, demanding that God show him why he's experienced such evil when he's only done right.

Other prophets, including David, seem to have discovered that God cares more about the intent of your heart than an outward show. Despite their attempts to change public perception, the common notion of a righteousness determined by deeds prevails all the way through Jesus' time (and persists today!).

So the "paths of righteousness" in Psalm 23 instantly draw a picture of God leading you on a road where you can do no wrong. He'll surround you with so much goodness, you can't make a mistake. Instead of goodness coming from the inside out, it attacks you until it penetrates your soul. Every possible decision is right.

He'll do that so the world can see the true beauty of His character. That's what "for His name's sake" means. Ancient Hebrew names don't just identify one person as being different from someone else. They express the reputation of an individual. When you let God take care of you, the world watches to see how you'll act. God's reputation is at stake. And He loves drawing the world closer to Him by showing His goodness through you.

Up until this point, God's led you as a gracious Shepherd. It's still your responsibility to follow Him. Now match the first three verses against the second three verses, where the first verse compares to the fourth, the second with the fifth and third with the sixth. God's not just ahead of you. He opens Himself to as much intimacy as you can handle. When enemies and death surround you, He doesn't run in fear of His life, like a hired shepherd would. He walks through with you, making sure you don't get scared. Instead of leading you to a field and stream where you can eat and drink on your own, He brings an abundant feast to you, honoring you in front of the ones who tried to destroy you. You don't have to fight the battle. You don't have to vindicate yourself. Just leave it in His hands. God knows how to make you feel honored.

He doesn't stop at helping you to be free from wrong, He overwhelms your senses with His goodness. He overflows your containers with more pleasure and abundance than you can handle. He brings it to you. He hunts you down and showers you with it. He commits to blessing you with His love forever. You can't escape.

God never wanted you to do the right things for Him. He shows His greatness by serving you, by doing more than you expect. The God of the universe has opened a rift in the cosmos so you can experience so much of His love you have to give it away, just like He does. If that's not what you hoped to find, maybe it's time to become a sheep led by a tender Shepherd. If you ask Him, He'll show you His definition of rest and peace.

Follow-up questions

1. What's the worst job you can imagine and why?
2. If The Actual God in all His Holy Glory took that job, got His royal robes dirty, sweat, and bled for you, what would you think about Him?
3. What's the most important thing in your life that you could do for God (think of a specific goal)? How would that affect Him?

The Window to Beauty

The Cornerstone of the universe,
The Light bursting from suns,
The joy in giggles of little ones,
The God who is,
Has pledged Himself to my every need.
How could I ever lack?

Oases of sustenance awaken these lips.
Purified waters offer thirsty, sweet sips.
His breath renewing, refreshing, a heart that knew mourning,
His hands paving roads where I can do no wrong,
The world grasping His tenderness,
My name etched on His fingertips.

Even in threat of death's foul grip, no terror could poison my gaze.
Love's eyes still my soul.
His fist could shatter a whole universe full of demon fangs.
How could I tremble?
How could I fear,
Knowing such power stays so watchful, so near?

Hungry eyes may encircle me with hate,
But He sets out a feast of abundance right in front of them,
Throat bathing in nectar,
Lungs filling with perfumed air.
Nothing I do could escape Your care.
Nowhere I could evade this treasure. You share
Yourself.
Never a list to avoid.
No shame, only joy
Unlocking the secrets of Your heart,
The window to Your beauty,

Our journey,
Hands entwined
Forever.

An Irrelevant Debate – Psalm 24

"Prove to me that God exists." "Convince me that God's relevant to my life."

Ever heard those two challenges? Maybe just inside your head? They silently ravage minds with doubt and skepticism. Out loud, they provoke heated debates.

Forget them when you read Psalm 24. Ancient cultures (and the writers of this psalm) couldn't have cared less about those issues. They never questioned the existence or relevance of the gods. They wanted to know which god controlled what and how to appease them.

In their minds chaos constantly threatened to overturn kingdoms and ruin harvests. Creation stories abounded of sea monsters conquered by a divine hero who established earth and created order. The earth sat upon the seas and was ruled by a collection of divine beings. They regulated everything, from the sun to the insects. Success in life hinged upon securing their favor.

So the writer(s) of Psalm 24 start by proclaiming that it's Yahweh, their national deity, who controls everything. In fact the original language reads more like, "To Yahweh belong the earth, the entirety of creation, and every person in it. God's the one holding all the power." This wouldn't have been a boring line. It was bold, audacious, and daring. It forces the audience to pay wide-eyed attention. They're saying, "All of your gods mean nothing. Here's the only One that's worth appeasing or knowing."

He's also the One who brought order and life to the world. He's the Hero who conquered chaos, made dry land, and allows us to enjoy its goodness. That's what verse 2 says. He controls every aspect. No pantheon of beings rules with Him. Yahweh alone reigns supreme over all.

So how can you get Him on your side? What qualifies you to even approach such an awe-inspiring being? Those are the questions that dominated the writer's/s' thoughts. That's what every ancient mind would have asked at this point.

Verse 4 says that you have to be innocent in all your actions (clean hands) and blameless in your intentions. You can't have offered the precious value of who you are (your soul) to worthless things (vanity or idols). You can't commit yourself and then un-commit. You've got to have one single purpose, a united heart.

A person like that doesn't just receive a trinket, they receive the source of blessing, and peace forever. Straight from the most powerful Being in the universe. Not only that, God will surround you with so much goodness, you won't be able to make a mistake. He'll rescue you from every outside attack on your heart and every evil intent from within it.

Sounds good, doesn't it? Now verse 6 throws something unexpected out before the music takes over. It says that this isn't just for the pure and spotless, who've never done anything wrong. It says that these are the characteristics of those who seek after, investigate, and long to come as close as possible to God. It's people like Jacob, who, though he deceived his brother, parents, wives, and in-laws, would do anything to receive the blessing of God. And God's not just going to accept your (and my) screwed-up-ness, He's going to change you and make you worthy to live where He is.

Now the instruments carry us off. That's what the *Selah* is there for. They've got to set a majestic mood. It's got to be so powerful that your brain starts thinking, "Something important's about to happen." Your spine tingles in anticipation. Your hair stands up. Eyes widen. It's about to get really good . . .

Get ready, get ready! He's coming to you! That's what verse 7 says. You thought you were trying to find a way to Him, but the King of all glory, all power, all miraculous wonder isn't waiting for you to become perfect. Here He comes. Are you ready? Do you see Him? Pick up your eyes and look. Quit sleeping. Open up, gates of the city! Prepare yourselves. Open up, you doors that separate cosmic, heavenly reality from physical earth. He's about to enter in to overwhelm your senses.

And then the people ask, "Who is this King of Glory?" (NKJV). And the singers and music respond, "It's Yahweh, the unstoppable One who wins every battle." The description "strong and mighty" and "mighty in battle" are attached to the name Yahweh here. Ancient peoples did that to signal what aspect of God's character He's using. So He's coming in His awe-inspiring battle array. He's just conquered every cosmic force out there, and He's asking you to join Him. Awe-inspiring and humbling all at once.

It's such a mind-blowing concept, they have to sing it again with two minor differences. The first is that it says "lift up" to the everlasting doors instead of "be lifted up." I'm not sure if they were writing that just for the rhythm or sound, or if it's describing a more voluntary opening the second time. You decide. Investigate and figure it out for yourself.

The second, and much more important (or maybe just more obvious), difference occurs when God's name repeats. It changes to "Yahweh of hosts" in the Hebrew, or "the Lord Almighty" as some English translations read. Now He's not just masterful in battle, He's leading all of creation. Every bit of His power wants to enter in to you, your city, your nation. There's no way you'll come out unchanged. If your physical body doesn't explode from the joy and terror all in one, you'll want Him forever and tell everyone about it.

That's what happens when you really want the God who lives. He comes to you. He changes everything. Now imagine a group of people all longing for Him and committing themselves to following Him together. Get ready. Your heart's beginning to align with the desire of the God who commands the universe. No more debating. No more choosing who's right. No more pretending that your choice makes Him real or not. He's here. Are you with *Him*?

Was it David or not?

It's debated as to whether David, or the school of writers that David started, wrote the psalms attributed as "of David." That line of thought includes other psalms attributed to Heman or Jeduthun or Solomon or . . . Throughout this book I've indicated this uncertainty by saying "the psalmist(s)" or "whichever authors wrote this psalm" in certain chapters. In others I've pretended to know definitively that David or a particular group of writers wrote that psalm in order to tell an effective story.

You could write a whole book series about the search for the original authors of the psalms (and there are more out there than one person could read in a lifetime!), but none of the ones I've seen have helped me to understand the meaning of each particular psalm. The truth is that no one knows because none of us were present 3,000 years ago. Please forgive me if you feel that I'm not being correct enough. I'm happy to risk being wrong if it helps you to understand and feel the heart of David's and the other psalm-writers' stunning work.

If you just can't get this nagging question out of your head, go investigate. Try to read all the books about it you can. Get your hands dirty in some archaeological digs. Pray for God's help in figuring it out (because He cares about the tiniest things that we care about). Write a book about what you discover and send me a copy. I'd love to find out the real story if it helps me know the living God even more.

Follow-up questions

1. How do you answer people who tell you to prove to them that God exists?
2. How pure does a person have to be in order for God to accept their worship?
3. What's your least important thing that God would care about changing for you if you asked Him?

Open Up, All the Earth

All the earth you see,
Every leaf you touch,
What fingers grasp,
What feet explore,
More than what the mind perceives,
Stormy seas roar,
Howling winds scream on mountain heights,
Plunge into valleys wet with rain.
Even the blackest cave resounds with His name etched in stillness.
Atoms vibrate witness with the thump of each heart.
We all belong to Him.

He breathed on us,
Plunged a foundation deep in the churn of oceans,
Called forth land,
Conquered the waves and made a place to stand
Before Him in the heights of perfection.

To those whose hands hold no deception,
Whose spirit seeks pure refreshment
From no other source but God's grace,
To the generation that desires His face,
Stretches to receive what only He can give,
Topples every distraction from their path,
His arms flow satisfaction and rest.
Goodness and a clean conscience radiate in their smiles.

Open your eyes, oh people of truth.
He's returning in strength to make all things new.
Lift up your hands to the mighty King.
He defeated all evil, let nations sing!

Open your hearts, you redeemed by His love
Bask in the blaze of the glorious One.
Lift up your voices and praise the King!
He commands all of heaven, and His glory all earth will see.

More Desperate Than an Unjust Cellphone Bill – Psalm 55

They've gone too far. You're not going to give up. You've just listened to your cellphone company tell you they won't give back the $200 they charged you for their mistake. The "customer service" manager keeps saying the same thing. You've got to get through to them somehow.

"You think I'm gonna pay for your mistake?

"You expect me to take responsibility for what *you* did?"

The operator pauses. "Well, let me talk to a manager to see what I can do."

Notice how you just repeated yourself? You said pretty much the same thing twice, using slightly different words. You talk like that for extra emphasis (especially when a company's allowing you to experience their poor customer service). It gets people's attention. David (or the writer of this psalm) uses the exact same technique to make his plea to God. He does it in the first two sentences and then repeats the same technique through the entire piece. (In fact, ancient poets did this constantly. They thought of it as rhyming thoughts, rather than sounds.) A melancholy backdrop of strings surrounds this psalm, riveting the focus of anyone hearing the meaning of his words.

He starts with . . .

Listen to this artfully crafted prayer. Don't avoid my request for your help.
Pay attention to me and respond to (do something for) me.

Or in other words, don't just politely hear my poetic sighings and descriptions. Don't let it sit around while you get to other things. Give me all your attention. Act on my behalf . . .

Because my enemy keeps talking, keeps pressuring me.
They pile their lawlessness, their anger, their hate on me.

My heart weeps. Death covers me up.
I shake in fear. I shudder under the threat of my demise.

I wish I had innocent wings. I'd fly to a quiet place,
I'd flee to solitary stillness, the breeze blowing the sand, filling my mind.

Strings play as he pauses, deepening the down mood. "Take a chill pill, David. Surely it can't be that bad." Of course, for David, it had been. Chased by the king. Betrayed by his friend. His wife given to another man. Pretty much the bottom of life's barrel.

Although he just wants to escape all the evil surrounding him, he starts the next section by asking God to intervene, not just for his own benefit, but to change the lives of everyone in the city. What used to be a place of safety and order has become chaos and danger. It's not like some enemy came in and terrorized them. This has infected people he thought were his friends, people with whom he'd sought the Lord . . .

I'm hurrying to my hideout from the windy storm and whirling tornado. Engulf *them*, oh, One I serve, and disrupt their united tongues. It's all injustice and disputes in the city.

All day and night they surround it. Chaos and sorrow fill its core.
Evil desire sits at the core. Deception and fraud never leave the streets.

Because it's not some enemy that disgraced me. I could have shouldered that.

It's not someone who hated me that stood to fight me. I would have hid from him.

It was you, my comrade, my mentor, my friend.
We shared dreams and conversations about God in His house with believers.

Let the realm of the dead seize them. Let the realm of the dead call their debt.
Let them descend alive into hell because evil has rotted them to the core.

As for me, I'm calling God. Yahweh saves me.
All day long I complain and make noise. He listens to my voice.

From the place of attack He pulls me to peace. They surrounded me in packs.
God will listen and pay them back. He's lived here since the beginning of time.

Whoa, there, David. I thought God was merciful? He is. But He doesn't let out-of-control evil run unchecked. When it's destroying the ones He loves, God acts. You don't want to be in the way. He'll remove the evil that threatens His children. If you hold onto it, it'll take you to hell with it.

I bet the strings either played something incredibly unsettling during that part or stopped completely to heighten the shock. Then they started strumming soothing tones. And finally returned to the beginning melody for the conclusion of the last section . . .

Those who won't change don't respect God.
He shook my hand in an oath of peace and broke his solemn vow.

His mouth slid out creamy smoothness, while his heart planned attack.
His words softened me like oil, and then unleashed their swords.

Throw all your burdens on Yahweh and He will take care of you. He never allows the righteous to fall.

And You, God, You'll bring bloodthirsty despots to complete ruin. Their life will be cut in half.

And me. I'm trusting You.

And the strings stop.

You're back on the phone, waiting for the "manager's response." "What am I going to do . . . ? God, I'm switching my allegiance from myself or the seemingly scary cellphone company to You. Please help me get this $200 back. You've been in charge forever. I'll trust that every word You say is true. I'll trust that You won't let me fall."

Peace washes your heart. You breathe deeply and let out a happy sigh. Even if they don't give you a full refund like you want, you know God's got your back. He'll come through with the money to pay your phone bill and everything else somehow.

The cellphone operator comes back on the line. "We've discovered that you were correct. We're refunding the $200 to your account."

Your brain starts wondering if you got the $200 back when you asked God, or if God already had sent the blessing and just wanted you to ask Him, so you'd enjoy the good news more. Either way, He doesn't give up on you. He's with you. He delights in making you shine.

Follow-up questions

1. What's the worst injustice that you've experienced in your life?
2. How does God determine who deserves mercy and who deserves justice?
3. What (if anything) can you do to make God bless you?

Escape, Rescue, and Safety

I wander long past midnight,
Find no comfort,
Pacing, churning, groaning,
Pricking, jabbing shards of glass in tender skin,
Between my toes,
Tearing fingernails.
Their words never end,
Hatred, pressure, looking for an excuse
To lock my prison,
Point their fingers,
Roll their eyes,
Contempt and traps, slurping poison plans,
Stabs of pain ripping a heart terrified.
Dismay hurls darts from every side.
Twisted thoughts, constant fear,
Darkness whispers, licks my ear.
If only I could make it stop,
Dreamless sleep
Surround my mind with the arms of clouds,
Cushiony soft and warm,
Where no one would ever find me.

Hear this voice,
A shaking plea.
My request won't leave.
Come and still the sea.
Make the striving cease,
Speak with justice,
Rain Your peace, oh God of all.

Whoosh me into shelter from the tempest's howling wind.
Swallow the din of my harassers.

Pulverize the violence of their contentious tongues.
They've tainted every city street,
Splattered violence,
Hungry for trouble,
Infecting each inhabitant with a lust for deceit,
Eyes that savor complete destruction.
The poor claw for bread.
Skin splits under snapping whips.
Feet bathe in innocent blood,
And that's the attitude at church,
Among my friends.
If it was my enemy I could take it,
But we sang songs together,
Shared secret prayers.
They smiled every word
While stabbing my back.
Give them their reward, God.
They've buried themselves in evil so deep,
Death is their due.
Every breath I have seeks You.
Hear my plea.
Rescue day and night.
You live to listen and save.

Hear my voice.
Crush my enemies!
Your word splits the seas
Long before my need.
Make the striving cease.
Speak Your justice,
Rain Your peace, oh God of all.

Nothing changes them anymore.
They don't care about God,

Betraying neighbors,
Flickering-tongued promises
Coiling to strike,
Fangs dripping intent,
Smooth and beautifully deadly.
Handle all my snakes, Creator of all.
Feed them frailty, destruction.
Parch their thirst for deceit and blood.
Dig an early grave.
Swallow their plans.
In Your tender gaze I forget their doom,
Sleeping deep and sweet,
Satisfied, protected,
Forever little feet walking safely,
Trusting only You.

Live Well or Die – Psalm 1

What image pops into your mind when I say the word "blessed"? Do you even have one? The closest I could get is the word "happy" or a smile. Yet I've had Psalm 1 memorized since I was five years old. I'd never thought about what the word "blessed" meant until now.

In the ancient world, being blessed packed a much bigger punch. In his book, *Ancient Near Eastern Thought and the Old Testament*, John Walton mentions that no concept existed of a righteousness apart from the deeds a person does until Moses unveiled God's covenant to the nation of Israel. You can't find it in archaeological texts or inscriptions in all the surrounding cultures.

Even then, being "blessed" primarily meant that everything turned out well for you. Your crops grew high. Animals reproduced. Financial deals made you wealthy. Calamities never destroyed anything you owned. When you spoke, people listened. People gazed out of esteem and envy when you strode by.

Start there when trying to grasp what Psalm 1's saying. It's not a guarantee that all those things will happen to you. But that's what will begin to overtake you if you pay attention to what it says to do.

First, avoid any of these three activities: 1) surrounding yourself with the advice of people who clearly aren't following God, 2) persisting in doing things that you know don't honor God, and 3) ridiculing everything others do while doing nothing yourself.

More importantly, make listening to God's word your greatest pleasure. Think about it throughout the day. Remind yourself of it as you fall asleep. The Hebrew concept of "Law" (translated from the word *Torah*) wasn't just the rules that determine right from wrong. It was the covenant God had given them to make them His own special people. When they thought about "God's Law" they reminded themselves of the love, care, and honor that flowed from God's heart.

Verse 3 paints a picture of a majestic tree planted in a garden with rivers of water nourishing it. Even those of us today get the reference to the Garden of Eden, with four rivers that flow out from it. Ancient people also understood that a garden always grew next to a temple, a home for "the god," which was most often built on top of a river, spring, or had some sort of moving water associated with it. They believed that the "god" would bring his or her presence to the temple and then walk in the garden with only the king or priest.

In the psalm, everyone who longs for God gets to live with Him in His personal garden. He'll nourish and feed us with His refreshing streams. He'll protect us from danger; pour His favor down on all our steps. He'll surround us with Himself.

Contrast that to the dried up, rootless picture of what happens to those who set themselves against God. They get blown to and fro with every circumstance of life. Jesus' audience no doubt connected His parable of the person who built his house on sand with Psalm 1. He equated hearing and not obeying God's word with the same wickedness that fights against God to destroy His people. Kinda serious! He also made His teaching equal to the covenant God had made with Israel. An extremely bold claim for a human!

Without roots or nourishment, there's no way that someone could stand with those who love God when the storms of life blow. How could you hope to endure the judgment of a God who sees to the core of your soul? Is there any way to get out of the "wicked" group of people and into the "righteous" group?

It's interesting that it says that the Lord "knows the way of the righteous." The word "know" in Hebrew is *Yada*, the same one used for "and Adam knew his wife." It's intimate, full disclosure. God's idea of righteousness is determined by closeness to Him and obedience to what He says, not just external goodness or circumstances.

Try delighting yourself in God. Leave the circle of people who just criticize others. Don't surround yourself with wickedness. Move toward the God who loves you. Ask Him to give you the desire if you don't "feel" it. He'll actively draw close, love, protect, and open up the secrets of His heart to you. He'll surround you with His blessings and goodness like a shield and nourishing stream all at once.

Those who fight against God have no such help. Everything about them ends.

Follow-up questions

1. What are some of the ways God has blessed you? (Try to list at least five.)
2. What makes people think that God in the "Old Testament" is different to Jesus?
3. How bad do you have to be to end up like "the wicked"?

The Choice

I wish I could describe the bliss,
The taste of an innocent kiss,
A smile unburdened by pain,
Breathing gulps of joy with no stain of regret
For swallowing selfish advice,
Or planting your feet in a heart of pride.
It's so much better to choose courage over mocking everyone
    else's life.

Let the character of God brighten your eyes.
Fill your belly with goodness until darkness dies.
You'll find nourishment and health, rising through bones,
Strengthening muscles, growing past failures and fears,
Giving in abundance through every season,
Pouring out hope,
Unstoppable compassion,
Love with no expectation of return,
A new garden that fills the earth.
It could all be yours,

Or you can watch it disappear like smoke on the breeze,
Grasping at emptiness,
Silence answering pleas for mercy,
The end of a self-indulgent life.

He who lives opens all He is to those who choose Him.
All who choose themselves find death.

Everyone Lies – Psalm 12

Search the internet. Watch the news. You're surrounded by liars and phonies, cheaters, and thieves. People post what they want you to see on Facebook and keep their shame behind closed doors. Celebrities vomit out their rants on Twitter while gulping down decadent lives funded by faceless masses. One by one our heroes fall, even those who seemed so dependable, so pure. Everything secret eventually comes to light. Is there anyone who tells the truth?

Apparently it wasn't any different in the time when Psalm 12 was written. "Help! Good people fail. The pillars of society vanish," the writer(s) say in verse 1. "Everyone talks about worthless rubbish with their friends. They use slippery language, double motives to twist their words to mean whatever they want," verse 2 continues.

Sounds pretty familiar. From kindergarten right through to the business world, those around you manipulate and mistreat you and anyone else in their way as they climb the social mountain. The only things that change are the clothes they wear and the power they wield.

God takes the words you say and the way you treat others very seriously. "He'll cut out all your slippery language and every tongue that talks like it's got it all figured out," verse 3 warns. You can see the knife slicing inside someone's mouth. Gross.

Just to be clear, this isn't if you accidentally say something prideful. Verse 4 tells us that they've internally decided that they're going to use their words to do what they want and no one will tell them what to do. If you've decided that, you probably wouldn't be reading this book. If you recognize any of your actions and words coming from that attitude, God's merciful arms long for you to come to Him, confess your wrong, and accept His power to change. Know how I know? Look at what God says Himself in verse 5 . . .

"Because of the destruction of the poor, the pleas of the oppressed, I Myself will show My strength." With the mention of the name Yahweh, the original listeners would have instantly recalled God's miracles that rescued them from being slaves of the most powerful kingdom on earth and guided them to a land of their own. They would have remembered how patient He'd been, despite their complaining and faithlessness. They would have remembered His unchallengeable might.

God will give the lowly the safety for which they yearn. That's just like the three little pigs in a brick house with a wolf trying to blow away bricks. Read how the King James Version puts the end of verse 5: "from him that puffeth at him." The Hebrew word is *puwach*. Just try to say that. You have to blow air out just to make the sound. Good luck trying to scare God by blowing at Him. To Him all those evil people's words are simply hot wind.

You can depend on the words God speaks. Verse 6 says that you can trust Yahweh's words like the purest silver. The way you purify silver is by melting it in a ceramic kiln. That means the temperature has to reach 1,764°F (962°C). When that happens, the impurities float to the top and either get poured off or are attracted to the crucible.

The ancient method of purifying silver is still the way to get the purest silver. Now imagine purifying it that way seven times. In fact, imagine purifying it infinitely, because that's what ancient writers meant when they used the phrase "seven times" to refer to a process. We can't even imagine the purity of God's intentions when He speaks. Unlike humans, He has no mixed motives. When He says He'll rescue you when you call, He means it.

Now we've seen three sets of statements: Verses 1–2 expose the problem; verses 3–4 offer a human answer; and verses 5–6 deliver a quote from the Almighty Himself. Finally verses 7–8 sum it all up:

"God will place Himself as a protective guard over those who call on Him. He'll stay from now through the rest of eternity. As for those who make themselves their own master they go in circles. You'll see them all around you, trying to win the help and trust of completely corrupt people. They sell their integrity to look good in front of mere humans."

So choose. Would you rather depend on One who only speaks truth and sets all His power to give honor to the lowest of the low? Or do you want to climb your own mountain, like a dung beetle trying to stand on top of the biggest ball of poo? I want the arms of the God who loves me. I'm pretty sure you want 'em too.

A song of eight

The inscription at the beginning says this Psalm was "To the chief musician upon Sheminith (eight), a psalm of (or to) David." This was a song. Maybe it was on a harp of eight strings, or maybe it was eight lines sung over and over again, each one played on a different string. Try meditating on each verse. Put them together into groups of two and see what you learn. Say them aloud. Sing them. Put them to music. With each approach you try, you'll find yourself seeing more and more of God and how good He really is.

Follow-up questions

1. How often do you lie? (Even remembering something incorrectly counts!)
2. At what time in your life have you had the purest motives?
3. What specific thing(s) would you be willing to give up to have a pure desire for God?

Searching for Honesty

I don't know anyone who doesn't lie.
Faithfulness isn't cool unless it gets us a bigger slice of pie
To savor on our double tongues,
Flicker, flicker, twitter, twitter but not a word of substance,
Nothing more than a political merry-go-round
Spinning faster and cleverer,
Correct and sensitive,
Never honest or bold enough to take a stand,
Endless movement, the thrill of excitement,
But no transportation to an awaiting feast in the promised land.

Some day we'll get off this ride,
Smell the burning of our polite, hollow promises,
Mixed motives, hidden intentions.
The Holy Judge of the earth takes seriously every careless vow,
Tears out poisoned tongues, so proud and full of ourselves!
Have we lost the ability to really speak?
Have our words become so weak
They can't defeat enough pride to say, "I was wrong?"
We belong together, no matter how wide the chasm of our
    opposing beliefs.
We've been straining so hard it's impossible to see
How our illusion of control robs us of life until the day we die.

I know Someone unable to lie
Whose heart pours out faithfulness from before the birth of time
Who says, "Now, I will arise.
For the end of injustice,
For the groans of prisoners locked in desperate chains.
I'm a fortress you can always run to.
I'm the peace that will never leave you.
I've heard every whispered tear of hope all alone in the night,

And I haven't been sleeping,
Or bored,
Or robbed of My heart of compassion.
My hand can pull you out from the darkest, suckingest black hole
    that crushed your dreams."

Test His truth.
See if He won't answer.
Find the flaw in His eyes of love
If you dare to expose your own heart to His reflection.
God watches over all who call on Him.
He knows how to keep tender hearts alive,
Create hopeful stars unafraid of time.
Whisper joy when all that surrounds are ravenous eyes
Eager to swallow their next piece of flesh.

Are You Willing to Go Insane? – Psalm 34

Saliva drips down your face. Splinters of wood collect under your fingernails. You'll have bruises on your shoulders and hips from all the walls you've rammed yourself into. The guards shuffle you toward the king. Your own king has every one of his soldiers hunting to kill you, and this king is your people's sworn enemy. "Please, God, let him think I'm actually crazy."

Through tangled hair and ravings, you see the shock on the enemy king's face . . .

"Can't you see this guy's insane? Why'd you bring him to me? Do I need another fool? Get him out of my house!"

The soldiers toss you out the gate. Still foaming at the mouth, you stagger off until you're out of sight. Then you fall to your knees, exhausted, thanking God for your escape, before running off to hide in a cave.

Whether this psalm was actually written by David or writers after him, it references the story of David pretending to be insane at the beginning. The psalm itself baffled me for a long time. I couldn't find a "followable" pattern until I realized that it's an acrostic – each line spelling out the Hebrew alphabet in order. Then I realized that verses 1–11 parallel verses 12–22. Of course you can read it in order, and it's great that way. But the secret comes when you compare each verse in the second half to its corresponding verse in the first half. Let's try it.

Verse 1: "I will kneel to adore Yahweh at all times. His *tehillah* will continually be in my mouth."

Verse 12: "Do you want to delight in life and love each day, seeing its good?"

Want to delight in life and see good every day? Kneel before God in worship, and let Him fill your mouth with His *tehillahs*. As we've already seen that word *tehillah* has been translated simply as "praise" or a "song," but it means much more. This was the same word used when Israel rejoiced after crossing the Red Sea. Moses used it a couple more times in telling Israel to remember all God's miracles. David sang it when he brought the ark to Jerusalem and dedicated the tabernacle. Jehoshaphat and Israel sung it as their battle strategy and routed all Moab and Ammon. Nehemiah says that they set up singers in place all day and night to sing *tehillahs*, just like David and Asaph had long ago. So what are they?

They start with the root word, *halal*. That means an individual celebrating loudly, even foolishly. It's actually the same word used for the shining light from a star. The idea is that you are praising God so brightly that the whole world can see.

Now imagine a whole bunch of people, add God's Spirit descending on them, giving them words and melodies, visions, and joy and you get *tehillah*. It's an ecstatic outpouring of song and emotion, most often in a group, inspired by the actual presence of Yahweh. If you've got that in your mouth every day, you'll see good for sure.

Verse 2: "My deepest soul will *halal* in Yahweh. The humble will hear and rejoice."

Verse 13: "Guard your tongue from evil and your lips from speaking treachery."

Want to keep your tongue from evil and your lips from treachery? Go nuts for God. Dance and shout as joyfully and wildly (without hurting others or yourself) as possible. If people see you and think you're a bit mad, that's fine. You'll have joined the company of famous kings, prophets, and Jesus. When the downtrodden and oppressed, the humiliated, and the really humble people see you, they'll glimpse hope and encouragement. Your joy will tug at their hearts. You'll make their day.

> Verse 3: "Oh, celebrate Yahweh with me. Let's give His reputation the highest fame as one."
> Verse 14: "Turn away from evil and do good. Search for peace and chase after it."

Want to stay away from evil and walk toward peace? Celebrate God and make Him famous together with other believers. He'll pour out rivers of peace on you. In fact, He'll turn you into a river that chases other people down to refresh them with God's peace.

> Verse 4: "I sought Yahweh, and He answered me and snatched me away from all my terrors."
> Verse 15: "The eyes of Yahweh point toward the just and His ears to those who call for help."

If you seek God, He'll answer and rescue you from everything that's hunting you down, even if it's inside you. In fact, He's waiting and actively listening for even the slightest peep or muffled cry that escapes your lips.

> Verse 5: "They look at Him and shine, and their faces are never ashamed."
> Verse 16: "The face of Yahweh cuts off the memory of those who do evil from the earth."

When you look at the Maker of everything, you'll see how He reacts to you. The joy in His eyes makes you smile. His arms open up to embrace you, his most precious daughter, his favorite son. You'll hold your head up with honor and confidence.

But God fights against those who set their heart to do evil, to oppress others, to take advantage of the innocent and needy. In fact, He'll wipe the memory of their existence from the earth. Yikes!

> Verse 6: "This afflicted man called, and Yahweh answered and saved him from trouble."
> Verse 17: "The just call out and Yahweh answers and snatches them away from every trouble."

He doesn't trample the broken. If you're broken, in need of repair, He longs to listen. He'll come running to rescue you from everything that's too strong for you.

> Verse 7: "The Spirit of Yahweh surrounds those who stand in awe of Him and draws their weapons for battle."
> Verse 18: "Yahweh stays near to the brokenhearted and saves the trampled spirit."

He'll make His camp to surround you, arming you for battle, taking care of your needs, and refreshing your soul. And then He won't leave. He'll stand with you, fighting alongside you as long as it takes to deliver you from your mess and heal your wounds, inside and out.

> Verse 8: "Taste and see that Yahweh's good. Happy is the warrior who hides in Him."
> Verse 19: "The just experience much evil. But Yahweh snatches them away from all of it."

If you haven't met Him, ask Him for a taste of His presence. Call on Him for help. Life's full of injustice and battles to fight, but He's the harbor that will shelter you, affirm you, and He will also wrap His arms around your vulnerable spirit. No tsunami's too big for Him to stop. No eddy's too small to ask for His rescue.

Verse 9: "Stand in awe of Yahweh, you holy ones. Those who do need nothing."
Verse 20: "He takes care of all his bones. Not one of them is broken."

Just look at Him and marvel. The One whose words pulsated the universe to life wants to nuzzle close to you. The God whose justice can straighten the most crooked of situations is full of mercy and forgiveness. If you keep your eyes on Him, He'll take care of everything you need. He won't let you be broken.

In fact, John used this particular passage in chapter 19 of his gospel to demonstrate that the Messiah was still being cared for by God while on the cross. Yes, Jesus suffered, but His spirit was never broken. And neither were his physical bones. He chose to endure the torture He experienced for the sake of those He loves. He's the perfect example of God's character lived out in a fragile human body.

Verse 10: "Young lions hunger and get famished, but those who seek Yahweh never lack good."
Verse 21: "Evil will kill criminals and those who hate the just will be found guilty."

Even the strongest among us experience days when we're weak. If you don't think so, just sing the Bill Withers song, "Lean on me, when you're not strong . . ."

Lean on the Maker of your soul. You'll never lack good. Criminals never lean on God. They have to provide everything for themselves. Those who hate the just refuse even the slightest help. It's why evil hunts them down, why they always end up guilty of the thing they hate. The only way you get included in that is if you choose evil over the goodness of God.

Verse 11: "Come, you sons, listen to me. I'll instruct you in the awe of Yahweh."

Verse 22: "Yahweh pays the ransom for the spirit of His servants. None of those who hide in Him will be found guilty."

You want to know what the "fear of the Lord" really means? Run toward Him when you're afraid. Even if you recognize how great and powerful He is and are terrified, draw near. He won't accuse you. He won't crush you. Even the parts you overlook are important to Him. He gladly pays the cost to rescue the souls of those who dare accept His offer to join His divine family.

Wow. Now think on the fact that it does all that and starts with the next letter of the alphabet in each line. It's one of the most masterful compositions in all of the psalms. Whether David wrote it while hiding out in a cave or someone else wrote it later in their own tricky situation, it's not a bad way to prove that you're not insane.

Follow-up questions

1. How big does one of your personal problems have to be for God to care about it?
2. When was the last time you sung a *tehillah* or even a *halal*? If you can't think of a time, when do you plan to do it next?
3. Try writing an acrostic poem. It doesn't have to rhyme. Just choose a word, like "love" or "supercalifragilisticexpialidocious", or the whole alphabet from A to Z. Then write one line that starts with each consecutive letter. Make it fun or serious, whatever you want, but make it all about one topic. Do it right now. Then share what you learned from the experience with someone you know (or post it on the Tree of Psalms website www.treeeofpsalms.com or Facebook page!).

Winning the Eyes of Yahweh

Armies couldn't stop my mouth from speaking.
Blessing leaps from these lips unceasing,
Chariots racing to proclaim unstoppable love.
Downcast eyes look up, spirits swell with glee.
Everyone lets loose free word associations, nonsense dances,
Festival bands filling eardrums, colors, chorus,
Galloping shouts of praise to the glorious King,
Hope of every living thing.

I let loose the faintest whisper, and He came near,
Jump-started my heart from fear,
Killed darkness and caused my face to shine.
Look in His eyes and drink release from condemning lies.
My final breath had just escaped my chest, and He plunged
     through waters of death to make me stand.
Not only rescuing one time. He pitched His camp,
Overwhelming my heart with liberation,
Petals of sweetness caressing my tongue,
Quiet, happy heart beating in this little one who looked to Him.

Risk your every desire in His affectionate arms.
See how His heart undresses for all who seek His love.
Tigers suffer the pangs of need,
Under the Father's wings waits a lavish feast.
Venison cranberry truffles,
Wine bottles uncorked,
Xylophone wedding bells ring,
Yesterday's sin lost in the song He sings,
Zero lack of any good thing.

Do you want to know the secret to life that lasts?
Smiles brimming with never-ending satisfaction?

Humble your heart.
Draw near.
Listen, precious child.
Let these words train your feet in the fear of God.

Avoid anything anywhere close to a poisonous tongue.
Build bonfires of kisses to the Father, your lips dripping truth.
Choose goodness over the glistening fruit of evil.
Dare to seize peace.
Each innocent act wins the eyes of the King,
Finds His ears open and listening.

God sets His might against all who savor injustice,
Hacks their memory out of the garden of existence.
If they would only cry out to Him, He would hear.
Just the slightest, struggled sound, and He rescues.
Kindness pulling minds from the swamp of despair,
Love lifting burdened spirits,
Multiplied compassion wrapping scared souls up in safety.
Nestle in His arms and lose your anxious thoughts completely.

Oh, the security of secrets in the Father's confidence,
Protection from the most tortured, frightened past,
Quelling internal strivings in the deepest mountain fastnesses,
Restoring hope for healing that lasts,
Satisfied desire in hearts that ache for His love.

Terror swallows the dreams of those that lust for its power,
Useless in the desolation of their withered, youthful bower,
Vindication for the humble who run to the Lord's strong tower.
Whenever they call He buys back their soul.
X-rated pasts He cleanses white as snow.
Yahweh protects all who yield Him their trust.
Zion the home that erases all memory of loneliness.

More Personal Than What You Want – Psalm 17

Think about the idea that God cares about you personally. Whether you agree or not, a personal relationship with God gets the most attention from religious books, songs, and sermons of Western culture. All of the psalms most popular to us reflect a personal connection with God (Psalm 23, 139, 51, etc.). Maybe we're self-centered. Maybe technology's to blame. Maybe there's nothing wrong at all with that point of view, and it's just the unique way *our* culture looks at the world. It's not the same in other cultures. It wouldn't have been the case in David's time.

To the nations surrounding Israel (and most of Israel), gods were national, local, or ancestral. The idea of a national God caring about one individual seemed absurd. The idea of an ancestral god being powerful enough to build a nation out of one family (Abraham and Sarah) and then show his or her might over all the other gods (the Egyptian plagues and Israel's deliverance through obvious miracles) had never been conceived before Moses. In fact, I can't think of another nation in all of history that can tell a story like that. Yet that's exactly what had happened, starting with Abraham and culminating in David's kingdom.

The people of Israel had such a difficult time processing this personal view of their national God that they still held on to their family gods. Archaeological digs have revealed idols in Jewish houses all the way up to their exile to Babylon. They possessed the Law and the Ten Commandments, but only a select few ever got the chance to read them. It was mind-blowing for David (or the psalmist dedicating this to David's style or memory) to address God so intimately.

He starts in verses 1 and 2 by putting himself at the mercy of Yahweh righteousness, the name given to indicate that God was going to dispense justice. "Take action on my behalf. Hear my request. I'm not trying to hide anything from You. When I stand before you, you look straight through me. You could figure out who's to blame from nineteen centuries of a national feud," he seems to say. Sounds like a pretty official request so far.

But then in verse 3 he starts to get personal. "You've investigated my heart. You visit me at night." What? What kind of God is this? Relax. I think what David's saying is, "You even know what happens in my dreams." "Put me on trial and see that I've planned no evil," he says. "I haven't said anything that's wrong." "If you want to look at what I've done, it's Your words that have kept me out of criminal activities."

It was no joke for David to say that God's words had kept him from being a criminal. When he fled from Saul, he was surrounded by them. 1 Samuel 22:2 says that "Everyone who was in distress, everyone who was in debt and anyone who was discontented gathered to him." He had opportunities to kill the king, but he didn't. He could have kept all the spoils of his raiding to himself and his men, but he gave them to the cities surrounding him. He kept worshiping Yahweh even when he lived in the land of the Philistines or when men from other nationalities urged him to try out their gods.

After what seems like self-justification, David rolls out his request in verse 5: "Keep me supported and firmly entrenched in your ways so that I don't become unsteady." Notice he's not asking for God to decide his court case versus someone else. He's asking for all of God's power to keep him close to God's heart. He can't do it on his own. He needs God to keep him honest.

How often are you concerned about your own welfare? You need enough money or want others to perceive you as successful. You want physical healing. You want people to treat you better. What your heart really needs is for God to keep you close.

It's hard to do evil when you're aware that the most holy Being in the universe is with you. And David, who came from a culture that had little to no concept of personal friendship with God, realized the same thing.

In verse 6 David expresses his confidence that he's got God's attention. "I know you're going to act on my behalf, 'cause that's who you are," he says. He doesn't call Him Yahweh. Instead, he refers to him as *El*, the generic term for God. It's like calling God his friend.

It gets more intimate in verse 7: "Show me miracles of Your faithful goodness and power you save for those who come running to You when they're attacked." You get the picture of a little boy or girl running to their father. Your enemies hate you. They're too strong for you. But your deliverer does miracles. He can part the sea. He can plunder the most powerful nation on earth and give it to you without you lifting a finger. He saves all that power to defend you when you run to Him.

With those seven verses, this psalmist probably could have finished, and we'd have a happy worship song, one that makes us feel like God's on our side. You live happily in your world. God watches over you and helps you as you do what's right. And whenever things get really bad, you can run to Him for help. But that's only the first half.

David starts the second half in verse 8 with a request that goes way beyond the bounds of normal and decent religion . . . "Keep me as the apple of Your eye. Hide me under the shadow of Your wings" (NKJV).

This verse literally says, "Keep me in the pupil of the daughter of Your eye." It's saying, "Make sure I stay in the center of the tender spot You have in your heart for me. I'm your little baby chick, and under your wings I don't have to fight."

Look at it in comparison with verse 1, and he's writing, "Yes, I have a just cause, and I want you to act because I'm honestly asking for help, but I want to be closer. I want to be intimate with you. I want your love, your care, your tender affection, like a mother would protect her newborn child." The verse continues: "from the evil people that devastate me and hover, just waiting to gobble me up."

These aren't the words of a powerful person trying to impress a divine being. He's a little child telling his parent that the big kids beat him up and take his lunch money. He's saying, "Get close to me, God, because I'm the daughter, the son that you love, and these bad guys will kill me if they can."

Verse 10 sounds funny if you read the King James Version: "They are inclosed in their own fat." I immediately picture the world's biggest belly, locking someone by sheer force of gravity in a chair. I think what he's saying is, "They're comfortable being bad. They're set in their ways." And then he goes on: "Their words drip with arrogance." Notice how it's a comparison with the writer's "tested" and "tried" heart and innocent mouth in verse 3. Instead of finding good from the inside out, you can trace evil spilling from heart to mouth and to all their actions.

Verse 11 goes further. "They've got us surrounded. They look everywhere for us. Their appetite can't wait to gobble up anyone who's good and add them to their bloated stomachs." "My steps hold on to your paths," he previously said in verse 4. "But they're the ones who try to make me fall, intimidate, steal me from your ways."

But it's not some fat, bloated oaf on the hunt. Verse 12 says they're lions. They've honed their killing skills. Their appetite for evil stalks you. They surround you. You have no idea when they'll pounce. Ever been stalked by a pride of lions? If you're alone, your throat's about to be ripped by their fangs. They'll wrestle over who gets your intestines. The psalmist who wrote this wasn't talking about your little brother or sister who annoys you, or the assistant at the store who doesn't seem to like you. He's talking about a murderer who can't go to sleep at night without planning new ways to make you suffer a slow death.

Verse 13: "Get up, God, confront them and make them submit to You. Deliver my soul by introducing the wicked to Your sword."

Nothing stops someone who's sold themselves to evil like that other than God's sword. It's the "baddest" weapon on the planet. It doesn't just slice and dice. It vaporizes. He speaks, and the most ruthless dictator pees his pants. When you ask for God's deliverance, He'll go look your enemy in the face, make Him bow, and, if He has to, take him out. You get to be the vulnerable bird who watches momma eagle unleash her beak and talons on the threat to her baby.

Verse 14: "Deliver me from mortal men, from humans who get satisfied with temporary treasures in this life." They're just humans. Their power only lasts in this world. But the God he's petitioning lasts forever. What a relief. What rest you find when that much power waits to save you and beckons you close!

Notice that I left off the second half of verse 14. That's no mistake. If you look at the original Hebrew it uses the word translated into English as "hidden treasure," or "temporary treasures," as I've translated it, twice. It didn't make sense to me that it gets included with verse 14, as if God would satisfy the wicked with children and so much abundance that they can give it to their children after them. Why would he give them what they don't want?

Yes, God is that good, but in this psalm, David's contrasting the wicked, who get their jollies from worthless and temporary things, with the righteous, who understand that God's real treasure is people, children, future generations, leaving a legacy. I believe he's actually summing up verses 1–7, saying that when you call for God's rescue, He'll save you, establish you, give you a future that goes beyond your life on earth, and give you so much abundance in this world that you have to give it away to others. That would make the second half of verse 14 to read as "The righteous (they) are fully satisfied with children and leave an inheritance to their little ones."

But then he's not done. Rabbi Benjamin J. Segal, in his commentary on Psalm 17, points out that "Last verses are often a surprise in the Psalms, and that is most certainly the case here." He understands Hebrew way better than me, and I was relieved to find that he thinks the same thing I do about this psalm being written in two halves with a wrap-up verse. Look at how he translates verse 15: "Then I, justified, will behold Your face; awake, I shall be sated with the vision of you."

"No one has seen God at anytime," John says in the New Testament (John 1:18; 6:46). "No man may see My face and live," God Himself tells Moses in Exodus 33:20. But here the psalmist says, "If You justify me, God, I'll be able to look You straight in the face. All Your beauty, all Your glory will be exposed to my eyes. Even better, I'll be able to really see. I'll be awake for the first time. Nothing on earth could ever satisfy my longing, but when I look in Your eyes I'll finally know fulfillment."

Just take a moment to think about that. Close your eyes. Look at God's beauty. Ask Him to let you see His eyes, His smile. You can't see Him without Him seeing every part of you. And when you see His response, the way looking at you affects His emotions, it will change you forever.

Even in a culture that doesn't dread omens in the sky and the threat of God's power, that's a shocking request. I can't imagine how it blew the mind of any ancient ear it entered. The Creator of the universe wants to unveil His beauty to change you. Are you ready to meet Him?

Do you just want what you want? Or do you dare allow God into the intimate places of your soul? Into the memories you're scared to show anyone else? To be the only protector you can really trust? David and the writers of the psalms seemed to know what really mattered thousands of years ago. Maybe the God he encountered still knows how to make Himself relevant today.

Follow-up questions

1. Why do you think that the psalms that are the most personal are the most popular ones in Western culture?
2. Who on the earth today or in the past fits the description of the evil people in the second half of this psalm?
3. How would you celebrate if you found out that God loves you more than you could imagine, has rescued you from every enemy, plans to give you more goodness on earth than you can handle – and will continue it past your lifetime?

Painted Picture

I could paint You a picture, but
You know my heart.
You made it.
You breathed it to life.

I could send You a message,
Nothing fancy,
Nothing sneaky,
Nothing but my prayer to You.

God of everything just and true,
Let my cry find Your weakness,
Your soft spot to defend me,
See the good parts of my heart.

Late at night, in stillness
I felt You searching my thoughts,
Testing my lips.
You've made them gentle,

You sent Your word,
Keeping me from destruction,
Not letting me stray,
Not letting me slip.

Oh, I know You hear,
You can't help but act
As this picture shouts,
This message groans,

I want to feast on the desire You spend,
How Your strength rushes to tenderness,

How You break the arms of wicked men
Who oppress the children You love.

Sometimes I just need to hide.
Sometimes I can't look outside,
Sometimes I need to know Your eyes
Can't find anything more beautiful than me.

Don't let my spirit get crushed.
Don't let their teeth taste my blood.
All around violence lurks,
Lions ready to rip flesh.

Hunters hide in the darkness.
Scavengers trail at a distance,
Mocking my weary resolve,
Shutting their ears to my plight.

Make them fall.
Shove their faces in the dirt.
Fill their mouths with broken teeth.
Sink Your sword in the heart of my enemies.

They possess only what they see,
Have no clue that You give
Every treasure that flees
The final close of their eyelids.

Don't let me forget.
I'd rather see You than know safety,
As long as You place me
Close to Your chest.

Make my life Your message,
My body Your masterpiece,
Your face filling every reflection,
A painted picture aglow with You.

When the Screwup Became King – Psalm 18

How do you celebrate? What's the biggest party you can imagine? President Obama's second inauguration was attended by 700,000 people. A million braved the rain for Queen Elizabeth's Diamond Jubilee. Psalm 18 was David's speech at his coronation. Just the men fit for military service in attendance numbered over 1.5 million.

David had gone from lowly shepherd to king of a nation, from pretending insanity in front of rulers to having everyone celebrate and bow to him. Unlike our current leaders, David didn't just give a speech, it was a song with him dancing. David truly must have been a rock star / warrior / king. Imagine you were there . . .

You've just arrived in Hebron to celebrate the crowning. It took three days to come all the way from Naphtali, but you made it. Camels, donkeys, and way too many sheep fill the air with bleating and all too familiar smells. Your clan's carved out a place a little off to the right and a third of the way from the front. Your eyes scan the sea of humanity that stretches from horizon to horizon. "There's more people here than I know numbers," you think.

Everyone starts quietening as some huge, burly guys clear the road up by the stage. Drums start beating. Trumpets blast. "The king's coming! The king's coming!!" the royal herald cries. "Here's the man who took down Goliath. Here's the one that Samuel anointed. He's Yahweh's chosen. He's slain his ten thousands. It's DAAAA-VIIIID!"

David strides to the stage, quick and light on his steps. "This guy looks smaller than the conqueror I've heard of," you think. Still, you can tell by his energy that you wouldn't want to mess with him. He moves like poetry.

The crowd turns silent. Every eye in the whole nation rivets on this one man. But pretty soon nobody cares about him. David focuses their attention on something else . . .

I'm passionately in love with You, Yahweh! *You're* my strength!
Yahweh my secret hiding place.
The One who delivers me.
My personal God.
My place where I go as a refuge.
My shield and defender!
My horn that pushes everything out of the way and rescues me.
My fortress that no one can conquer!

The music cranks behind him like a wailing organ behind a preacher in a little gospel church. As he finishes, the millions of people who've gathered go nuts and cheer like nobody's business.

"Yes!" you think. "If we've got a God like that with that many different powers, we can't lose! Huh. He didn't talk about any of his own accomplishments. That was unexpected, but this is gonna be great."

The music switches to a serious melody, and David starts to explain each name of God in order, starting with "my secret hiding place."

When I praise and call on Yahweh, He saves me from my enemies. It got bad, real bad.
(The music becomes scary and uncomfortable.)

Death grabbed hold. Floods of evil frightened me. The underworld wrapped its claws around me. Death traps stood in my way.

In that tight spot I called to Yahweh, my personal God, in desperation. He heard my voice and listened to my plea in His home, His royal presence making me close enough to whisper in His ears.
(The music quiets down with a ringing tune.)

You let me into Your cosmic palace like I belonged there. You give me an audience and let me up onto Your lap to say it in Your ear.
(The ringing tune repeats as the lyric repeats.)

"Into his ear? Nobody gets to do that with a god," you think. "What's the great Yahweh gonna do?" The music gets quiet for a second . . . but then explodes in anger, notes flying at you from all sides.

The earth cracked and reeled. The depths heaved. Mountains trembled. You turned red hot angry!

David yells, twirling and dancing.
"Here comes the Great Deliverer!" you shout, before realizing it was out loud. Everyone around you turns and hushes you.

Smoke curled from His nostrils! Fire from His mouth licked up everything in its path. He burned it all to lava hot coals. He ripped open every barrier between the cosmic world and earth and stepped in, His feet covered in mystery.
(The drums sync up with the trumpets.)

He rode on angelic beings. He flew on the wind. He had no fear of the dark and chaos. He pierced into thunderheads. He grabbed up their power and turned hail into coals of fire. He thundered with His voice. The Supreme Being puts hail and coals of fire in His voice!

You and the audience tremble as the music repeats to emphasize the awesome power of God.

Down came His arrows. His lightning made my enemies cry like little babies. You blew open the sea. You uncovered its depths with Your voice, with the blast of Your breath. God plunged Himself from on High and took me in His arms. They'd overcome me. I was too weak on my own. But all the chaos, the evil, the enemies that hated me were powerless to stop the Great Deliverer!

The band rocks out its celebration sound. David doesn't seem to care what anyone thinks as the sweat starts to show through his royal robes. You and everybody go nuts. (The music begins to soften.)

All those enemies swooped in for the kill when I had nowhere to go, just like Pharaoh and his army, but Yahweh became my staff. And He brought me to a safe, wide open place, with plenty of land, and set me free . . . just because He likes me. He does all this because I'm surrounded by goodness. He pays me back for having pure motives.
(The melody continues to soften and becomes a delicate tune.)

I followed Yahweh's ways. I didn't run away from Him to chase evil. I kept His law where I could see it at all times. I didn't forget His principles. I'm starting to look like them. It keeps me from even accidentally doing wrong. See what I mean about being surrounded by goodness, how He pays me back for having pure motives?
(The music returns to the beginning of the delicate tune and plays it again.)

With the kind, You show yourself kind. To those with flawless intentions, You reveal Your flawless holiness. With the pure, You show how pure You are. And with those who are twisted . . . You know how to wrestle.

"He's talking about Jacob!" you whisper to Ben-Naphtalet, your older brother, as you figure it out. He punches you to keep quiet.

You save the lowly. But You know how to make the proud lowly. You ignite my heart, God, my own personal God. You turn my darkness to day.

It's You who enabled me to run right through an army. My own personal God makes me fly over every barricade!

Shouting erupts as tears stream down everyone's cheeks. You don't know whether to dance or fall on your face weeping. People around you are doing both as the music washes over you. You're not ready to go on to the next names of God. "Just let me bask in this feeling for another moment." And then the music becomes slowly majestic.

The only God does everything perfectly. His words are the most refined silver. He shields and defends all who come running to Him. Can any other god really be called a God like Yahweh? Who else can you trust other than the personal God of all of us?
(The music quickens and delivers a majestic melody.)

God's the One who straps bravery on my heart. He blazes a pure highway for all my actions. He makes me as nimble as a mountain gazelle and lets me ascend to victory on the heights! He teaches me how to fight the enemy and makes my arms so strong; they could bend a bow made of titanium.
(The music goes back to the beginning of the majestic melody.)

You've given me Your personal shield and put all Your power into me. It's holding me up while Your humility spreads throughout my spirit. You're making my road wider and smoother. I'm standing without slipping.
(The music charges in your ears with drums and warlike sounds.)

I chased the enemies chasing me, caught 'em and didn't return home until they were no more. I shot 'em until they fell and couldn't crawl to their knees. They lie still under the heel of my boot. You made my enemies vulnerable. I destroyed everyone who hated me. They pleaded, but no one saved. They tried calling out to Yahweh, but He didn't answer them.

I pulverized them. They scattered like dust in the wind. I threw 'em out with the trash. You pulled me out of controversies and disputes and gave me honor like the most powerful nation on earth. Whole countries I don't even know have offered me their service. As soon as they heard about me, their ears perked up. All their children came cowering to bow down. They disintegrated in front of me and ran to hide, trembling behind their walls.

"Holy sheep, this is awesome! David's gonna be one amazing . . ." and the music stops. Everyone stops, stunned at the break in momentum. Then the trumpets, drums, strings and singers erupt together in the most majestic chorus yet. Your ears are gonna split with the sound.

"Yahweh's alive!" David shouts at the top of his lungs.
"Yahweh's alive!" you and all Israel shout back instinctively.

"All greatness be to my fortress, the Exalted One, my Personal God, the One who saves me!!"
"All greatness be to my fortress, the Exalted One, my Personal God, the One who saves me!!" you scream in your delirium.

"It's God who avenges me. He puts nations under me. He frees me and sets me out of reach of my enemies, even the ones inside me. You rescue me from every violent man. That's why I'm gonna tell everyone in the world about you, Yahweh! I'll sing songs forever about your character!"

David finishes screaming it out, leaps in the air, and starts the craziest, most powerful moves you've ever seen. The music takes off and everyone starts dancing. Sweat pours down your face. Your feet ache. Your calves start to tighten up from all the jumping. Ben-Naphtalet trips on your foot and falls over. You help him up and both of you start dancing again. Everyone keeps it up until the music winds down, you can't move anymore, and David stands in silence and stillness.

"HE exalts! HE exalts!!" David's voice suddenly rings out as the instruments and singers scream their loudest note. "He saves the king. He in his kindness decided to anoint David and to continue the kingdom through my sons for the rest of eternity!"

Everyone yells their loudest and jumps their highest. The music starts jamming. No one thought they could dance anymore, but you and they find the strength. It all builds to one final hurrah. The whole nation shouts. And then you fall down laughing with Ben and all your family and friends. You've got three days of feasting with cakes, fruit, pies, pastries, juice, meat, and wine, all provided by the king. A hand knocks you to the ground.

"That's for tripping me during the dancing, Simon," Ben sneers at you.

You tackle him in a wrestling match you have no hope of winning. He weighs twice as much as you, even though he's twenty and you're eighteen. Finally, your mom yells at you to stop. You hope that Elisabeth, the girl with the dreamy eyes from the field next to yours noticed your wrestling moves. Maybe your family and hers will eat fig cakes together for dinner . . .

Late that night, as you lay down to sleep, David's speech and the music steal into your mind. "God's *my* shield," you wonder aloud.

"You're gonna need Him if you wrestle me again," says Ben.

"I know, Ben, but notice how David talked about God differently? He didn't even mention any other gods."

"'Cause they're totally worthless," Ben scoffs and turns over on his mat. "Other gods can only use the wind, sun, or some other earth power. Yahweh uses whichever of 'em He wants."

"Ben, You said *His* name!"

"So, King David said it way more than I did."

"Yeah . . . Wasn't it crazy when David started telling us he was weak?"

"Didn't expect that."

"I mean he's the king."

"Not like any king I've heard."

"I know. I was like, what's he doing?"

"And then God swoops in to save him."

"Yeah, and when he said God blew open the sea . . ."

"Couldn't you see Moses raising His staff?"

"Then David says God became *his* staff."

"Never expected that. David's so cool!"

"God's freakin' awesome!"

"I love our God!"

"So, he must be saying that God wants to be with us like He was with Moses and Israel!" you think to yourself. "Ben, I thought Moses was special, like an intermediary between God and Israel."

"He was. But so is David."

"You don't think . . ."

". . . that we could use God's power like that? No way. You just wanna out-wrestle me."

"No I don't."

"Yes you do."

"No. I don't! Think about it. Remember when he said "with the twisted . . ."

"Oh my gosh, it felt like He was talking about me."

"Me too!"

"'Cause I'm not like those first three. Maybe Grandma was, but not . . ."

"You know that was Jacob, right."

"For sure! Maybe he's our great ancestor, but that guy deceived, manipulated, and talk about twisted . . . He married two sisters!" Ben whispers, motioning you to keep it quiet.

"But then He wrestled with God . . . and God let *him* win!" you choke out.

"Are you . . . crying?"

"No . . ."

"Are too . . ."

"Okay, a little."

"Don't think it's gonna make me go easy on you . . ."

"I don't care about that."

Tears begin to flow as you remember the feelings you had during the speech and you see Yahweh in a completely unimagined light.

"C'mon, Simon, let's shut up and sleep," Ben says, pushing you away.

You turn over, your mind still racing with music and imagery. "Could you really be my own, my personal God?"

Something warm inside, like a secret voice that sounds even better than David's, drops a reply in your thoughts. Your lips widen into a smile. Tears form under closed eyelids.

"I can't believe You'd tell me I'm so valuable, so dear to Your heart. Why would *you* descend out of Your cosmic palace to be near to a screwup like . . ."

The structure of God's names in Psalm 18

Here's an outline of how I divided up Psalm 18. It seemed to fit the list of names David proclaims in verses 1 and 2:

Verses 1–2: David declares Yahweh as his strength with His seven names/powers
Verses 3–6: God, my secret hiding place
Verses 7–17: God, my deliverer
Verses 18–30: God, my personal God
Verses 31–4: God, my place of refuge
Verses 35–9: God, my shield
Verses 40–44: God, my horn
Verses 46–9: God, my fortress
Verse 50: David returns to Yahweh, his strength theme from verses 1–2, and shows how God uses it to exalt a screwup like him and display His love and kindness forever.

Follow-up questions:

1. Do you think David and Moses had access to more of God's power than you? Why or why not?
2. Try listing as many characteristics (names) of God as you can think of? Which ones mean the most to you?
3. How special do you think you are to God?

The Rescuer, the Lover, Our God

I'm in love with You, God,
The source of my power,
Immovable rock,
Unscalable tower.
I can trust in Your strength,
Rest my hope in Your name.
Precious far beyond words,
Your great love keeps me safe.

A cold chill breathed on my neck,
Wrapped a bony finger around my spine,
Whispered loneliness into empty arms,
Sharpened its sickle and stood before me,
Grinning at the prospect of my death.
I shrieked, full of fear.
Save me, O Mighty One, if You can hear.
And He heard, faster than the speed of light.
Even my slightest whisper would have awakened His fury.

Earthquakes tore through once proud depths.
Mountains trembled with fright.
The anger of God rattled loose the skies.
Clouds swallowed up all light.
Fire and darkness, terror and gloom,
Heaven split. Justice approached.
Angels flew, bearing His chariot wheels.
The wind lent its speed to His heavenly host.

His holy intention no eye could perceive.
Black thunderheads cloaked all His ways,
'Til lightning ripped through the hearts of His foes,
Their evil consumed in His blaze.

Peals of thunder, the voice of all truth,
He spoke, and no power could stand.
They fled from the sting of His arrows' sharp points
Crushed by the strength in His hand.

I saw the oceans part for my feet.
He overturned immovable bedrock for my sake,
Changing the course of history with one breath,
Robbing the enemy of its power of death.
He stretched out His mercy,
Straight to my heart,
Pulled all the chains of depression apart.
Shattered its grip,
Undid its hate,
Broke every door so the weak could escape.

Whenever all around me collapsed, I heard their lies,
But the voice of God spoke stronger,
Led me into fields of bounty,
Rescued me because He couldn't shield His heart from
    loving me,
Crowned me with favor and guarded my ways.
Staying close to His presence
Satisfies a clean conscience with mercy that never fades.

I've stayed close by Your side,
Rejected the lures of my own tricky heart,
Life flooding with Your character,
Eyes fixed on Your commands,
Mind with no room for sin,
Rejecting each sick suggestion of selfishness,
Held near by the embrace of Your Spirit,
Life overflowing with favor and blessings too great
    to count.

When the Screwup Became King – Psalm 18

If I show kindness, You open Your heavens of mercy.
In my integrity, You shine with pure, holy light.
When I beam brightly, Your smile shouts joyful approval.
When I've grown twisted, You love me till I give in,
Burn my past book of sin,
Write a new identity that no crowbar could ever pry from my chest
  again.

It's the humble You rescue.
My own arrogant boasting crashes to earth every time.
Be the power in our engine.
Blaze a spotlight in every selfish hiding place.
With Your help I'll rout every army,
Conquer each obstacle,
Tear down the idols that loom in my path.

Oh, God, no other plan works, but Yours.
How could I trust in any other promises?
You've always protected me and everyone else who seeks You.
Show me anyone close to the God who lives.
Find a foundation that won't move even in F5 tornado winds.
Only God performs miraculous feats,
Constructs flawless plans,
Guides tender feet in His ballerina dance,
Defends the helpless with feeble hands,
Flexing His strength through my arms.

My prayers shelter and protect the weak,
Buttressed as all Your authority speaks,
Peace, humility, tenderness, lifting my head,
Capturing my affection.
There's no way to fall with eyes fixed on You,
Problems trampled in dirt,
Enemies crushed under heels,

Darkness powerless to stand
Against the tsunami power of Your love and will.

You've prepared me for mission,
Forever sealing my past,
Locking the liars in a tomb of defeat,
Tearing their tongues out,
Trampling their hatred in the dust of the street.
When they invoke Your name,
You're not fooled by their cries,
Condemnation sinks to the bottom of the sea and dies.

Petty arguments can't touch me.
Leadership and wisdom anoints me.
New family surrounds me.
Unity of vision, the hope of success
Any deceiver or fear sowing pest
Flees from truth's light,
While I snuggle in arms of rest.

It's always been You, the strength of my life.
Let the whole earth hear how You answer my cries.
You fiercely protect,
Make the wicked bow down,
Bring me to safety,
Beyond any attempt to steal the treasure I've found.

How can I thank You,
Dearest Lover of my soul?
Everywhere I travel, let Your glory shine forth.
I'm the one that You've sent
Clothed in all Your delight,
Precious far beyond words,
Your great love wins each battle I fight.

What Makes *You* So Special? – Psalm 87

"What makes *you* so special?"

Man, that's a nasty thing to say. You mostly hear it on playgrounds. Occasionally adults whip it at you in an especially insecure moment. What's the first response that pops into your mind? For me, it's "Nothing, I'm not trying to . . ." Maybe instead of defending yourself, you launch an attack of your own. "The fact that I'm better than *you*!"

For an ancient Israelite, it was all about tribe, clan, and ancestors. The more important your relatives, or ancestors, the more special your place in the social pecking order. Check out this conversation from an excavated piece of papyrus. Scholars speculate that it's an ancient story about a couple of Jewish kids at Shiloh for the feast of Purim in 1643BC, during Eli's reign as High Priest . . .

"My father's the chief of the Shaulites, one of the first five families in Simeon."

"Oh yeah, well, I'm a Levite, I'm gonna be a priest."

"A donkey priest."

"Shut up!"

"You carry everything on your shoulders."

"Better than not carrying anything."

"Donkey."

"Quit it!"

"Donkey. You come from Korah!"

The papyrus cuts off at that point. I'm guessing that's where they started throwin' down. (You're aware that I made that whole thing up so that you could imagine the scene, right? Okay, cool.)

Sitting in your living room, you read "Korah" and think, "what's so bad about Korah?" If you've read this part of the Bible, you probably whizzed right past "of the sons of Korah" at the beginning of Psalm 87. If you actually stop to consider it, you might think, "Ahhh, 'sons of Korah.' Guess they were some important guys."

Very few of us think, "Rebel. Cursed. Snuffed out by God. The ground opened up and swallowed him, his household, his possessions, and everything that belonged to him. How'd *any* of his sons become priests and leaders of temple worship?" Even fewer of us know the answer.

Somehow, despite Korah's journey to the center of the earth, some of his descendants survived. They were still part of the tribe of Levi, and Moses assigned them to priestly duty. They got to carry all the holy pieces of the tabernacle on their shoulders as they trudged through the desert. "Thanks, Moses." All the other priestly servants got to load theirs in carts. Worse, they carried the stigma of Korah's rebellion and death. It must have sucked to be one of the sons of Korah, until David . . .

King David didn't just take the Ark of the Covenant back to Israel and prepare to build the temple. He created a whole new format of temple worship. He created full-time jobs for priests as doorkeepers, caretakers, musicians, and singers. Guess who the singers were . . . Yep. Twenty-five of the psalms are attributed to them. It says in 1 Chronicles 9:33 that they were "free from other service; for they were engaged in their work day and night." All day long they sang, worshiped, and wrote songs. Sounds like a sweet gig to me.

The sons of Korah begin this song (Psalm 87) with "His foundation is in the holy mountains." In commentaries they mention that "Jerusalem sits on the top of a number of mountains, and so this references Jerusalem." Hmmm . . . As a writer, even if I was talking about Jerusalem, I'd want to get you thinking about God's cosmic home, the holy mountains where "the gods," but in this case *the* God lives. Imagine Mount Olympus, from Greek mythology, or something similar. God starts building His home there.

But then verse 2 says that Yahweh "loves the gates of Zion more than any other place Jacob lives in." Gates didn't just include the doors, but all the walls and everything enclosed by Zion. And Zion literally is the same Hebrew word as the one translated "landmark" – with a slight change in pronunciation. It made (and to this day makes) every Jew think of the mountain where the Temple (God's home) is built. Jacob was another way for them to say Israel, only it carried with it the idea of Jacob stealing his brother's birthright.

So consider verses 1 and 2 as a way to say that God started building His home in the cosmic mountains and then finished it on the physical mountain of Zion. It implies that this song is about birthrights. God chose Zion over all the other imperfect places in Israel. "Magical, wondrous things get talked about when people mention the city where God Himself actually lives," verse 3 sums up before the first section ends.

As the music plays during the interlude, your brain starts thinking how amazing it is that the One and Only God chose a place in Israel to live. "Man, it must be cool to be in the holy city itself." The symphony of notes makes you feel rich and majestic. Harmonies and solos merge with the instruments. And then a different sound begins the second section . . .

Now they start singing different names of countries and cities: Rahab, Babylon, Philistia, Tyre, Ethiopia (or Cush). You and me have no clue the images and history these names would paint in their minds unless we dig a little . . .

You might remember Rahab the prostitute who hid Joshua's spies in Jericho and saved herself and . . . That's a totally different Rahab. This one's used in a couple of different psalms. It's the term for the mythical sea monster that God defeated to bring order to the earth and create dry land. It's also a poetic way to reference Egypt, the mighty crocodile of the Nile River that God defeated to make Israel a nation. They had a god for just about everything. Their culture swarmed with adultery, sexual promiscuity, and STDs. In fact, one of God's promises to Israel when they left Egypt was that he wouldn't bring any of the "diseases of the Egyptians" upon them if they followed Him (all the symptoms mentioned correspond perfectly to crabs, herpes, etc. . . .).

"Babylon" isn't talking about Nebuchadnezzar and his empire, because it probably wasn't Israel's primary threat when this was written. Here, it calls to mind Ur and the city that Abraham left to follow God. Ur at that time celebrated the god Marduk, head of the Babylonian pantheon. Every home had additional family gods. Plus, it was the original "Sin City" of the ancient world. Put Rahab and Babylon together and people go, "That's the beginning of your ancestry? You're not so holy." The sons of Korah are singing, "You think we were born in Egypt and Babylon."

Then they follow it up by singing, "Hey, Philistia, Tyre, Ethiopia, all you countries around us who think you're better than us and want to make us your servants. Look at me. I was born in Zion, the place the Only God that matters decided to make His home. And when people talk about Zion, they'll say, this person and that person were born there. They're part of God's family. And the Supreme Being of the unverse is going to make sure that they're His children forever."

"Yahweh Himself is gonna take roll of every person in the earth and say, 'this one that one . . . this one here . . . was born in My house. They get all the honor that belongs to me.'"

❋   ❋   ❋

The music and singing begin washing over you again. This time it's regal and majestic mixed with sweet and soothing. You can feel your heart tugging you with God's tenderness. He's named you His own personal son, His own treasured daughter. Nobody can take that from you. It's the same thing that happened to these sons of rebellion who turned into singers that spend all their time in the residence of the

God who orders the universe.

When they start singing again it's just voices and flutes. It starts out tender and lovely.

All the life and beauty that springs from me, comes from You.

The music plays a little more and they sing it again. This time you hear,

All my life comes from the river that flows out from your temple.

The music rises a bit more and they sing it again. Now you tap into your own ecstasy of emotion, "I'm connected, we're connected to the center of God's heart. He's chosen me. He's chosen us. We flow with Him. Our beauty comes from Him. He makes us beautiful. He turns the worst stories into honor and glory. We're the treasured children of God. I'm the special child of Almighty God!"

Who knows how long it's been as the music finally stops. You walk out with the song still dancing in your thoughts. Your face shines with joy, so much so that you run into a big dude carrying a bunch of firewood.

"Hey, what makes *you* so special that ya think you own the whole road?"

"Sorry," you say with a smile.

But you can't stop the music repeating in your head, "You're born in Zion."

"You're born . . . in *Zion*."

"*You* . . . were . . . born . . . in . . . Zion."

Follow-up questions

1. What is the best thing you could tell someone about yourself to prove that you deserve honor and respect for who you are?
2. What in your past or family history disqualifies you from living out your dreams?
3. How much time does it usually take you to connect to the God of the universe?

People of God

(to the theme of "Another One Bites the Dust" by Queen, sorta . . .)

He builds His house in the mighty mountains
Out of everybody He chose us
To fill the world with His wondrous glory
We're the people of God
Crowd response: We're the people of God (repeat)

You got the blessings
You've got His name
You've been born into the people of God
You can tell it in the countries and the cities of the earth
You've been born into the people of God

He called you daughter
He called you son
You've been born into the people of God
You could try to make it better but it's already done
You've been born into the people of God

(drum solo)

(Back to first stanza first time; second time through continue on.)

All you singers lift up your voice
Musicians come and make a joyful noise
You're refreshing our tongues
With Your waters of life
All of our joy comes from You.

(Repeat entire piece once.)

Because You Don't Want Endless Thirst – Psalm 95

Sometimes you just need time with something to understand it. That's the way it was for me with Psalm 95. I read it over and over again. The first read was great. The second left me intrigued. The third promised new revelations. The fourth showed me that I still didn't grasp how amazing it was. I must have read it more than twenty times, before it changed me enough to connect to its story.

Is that your experience? How long does it usually take you to get "in a worshipful mood?" Does "a worshipful mood" sound like something you've never experienced? Psalm 95 offers you a plan for getting your mind, spirit, and body ready to snuggle close in God's lap. Of course that's not all it does. It warns us of what happens when we refuse to believe that the good things in our life come from God. But don't worry about that yet. Start with the fun stuff . . .

The psalm begins with a call to come singing and shouting to God, the strongest, most immovable rock who rescues you. Come into His presence with thankfulness, fully expressing it, even shouting it out with "psalms" as it says. "Psalms" could be substituted as poems, rapping, or singing, but, whichever way, the idea is to do it loud so that everyone can hear.

Nothing in there says anything about silent reverence. It's an unburdening of your heart, an exposing of your vulnerability, a remembering of what He's done. He's rescued His people from certain death, failure, depravity, addiction. This isn't a solo psalm. It's an invitation for the church to enter into the full expression of joy to the Lord.

After all, there's no one else who's as good as Him. He's the "great God, and the great King above all gods" (NKJV). Remember how I said that they rhymed thoughts? Since there aren't any other lines in between the repeat, the psalmist is cleverly saying that there's nothing to compare with God.

Look throughout the earth. No matter how deep you go, every part of the earth is in His care. No matter how high, He's right there. Every part of sea, dry land, to the full extent of things seen and unseen, known and unknown He knows it all. Nothing escapes His attention.

So come to worship, to be with Him. He's the One who made you. He's your God, the One in which you trust. When it says to bow down and kneel it quickly follows with a picture of us as sheep, a flock of lambs that He cares for and knows intimately. Indulge in the scenery of rest. Feel the peace of God aching to wash over you.

The whole psalm up to this point has been a description of how to enter the rest of God, how to live in His real presence. Do you want to know how to be completely at rest in your soul, body, and emotions? Here's the plan:

1) Be loud and joyful, thanking Him for everything He's done, shouting and singing and speaking out your gratefulness.
2) Let the realization wash over you of the vastness of His knowledge and care. Everything is His.
3) Get quiet and humble yourself in the realization of His awesomeness, your smallness, and His love for you.

Do this together with other believers and something amazing happens. You'll end up doing exactly what He asks and being the person He's made you to be. It's so powerful, it will begin to restore the earth. The psalmist could have stopped here, but to further heighten the importance of this plan of rest for the people of God, He continues with a contrast of what happens when you don't follow it.

"Listen," the psalmist says. "Don't be stubborn. Pay attention to what the Lord's saying." He makes reference to the "day of trial in the wilderness" (NKJV). It's interesting that He doesn't say "when I tested your fathers." He says, "when your fathers tested Me in the wilderness." They didn't believe that anything that God did for them was really God.

In fact, the words "rebellion" and "trial" in the King James Version are literally "Meribah" (meaning contention) and "Massah" (meaning tempting), the names Moses gave to the place where Israel contended about whether or not God could provide for them and whether He was with them or not. That's where God told Moses the first time to strike the rock and water would come out. It also should remind you how the second time Moses was told to speak to the rock, and when, in his anger, he struck the rock again, God told him that he wouldn't enter the Promised Land. Big mistake.

Rest wasn't just a break from work. In ancient times, a god was said to take his or her rest after a temple was built and the god came to live in it. God wanted to give Israel the privilege of living in His holy presence, experiencing His favor, goodness, and love. But they refused to trust His character and get that close.

Psalm 95 says that though they saw God's work they still didn't accept His goodness. They wounded God's heart for forty years. They insisted on having something as a mediator, whether it was the Law, Moses, or a golden calf. They kept their hearts turned away from God and never gave thanks for all that God had done. God wouldn't profane His name by pretending that He was just like the other gods, demanding servitude rather than relationship. So God swore that they would never enter His rest.

It ends so suddenly. You feel like demanding a happy ending. But the way the psalmist wrote it should take you back to the beginning to say, "Whoa, so how do I enter His rest?"

Have you been expressing your thanks authentically: loudly, joyfully, and fully to the Lord, recognizing that He's God and basking in His care and love for you? Or do you proclaim that you're loving

Him on the inside but refuse to let it come out through your body and emotions? Have you seen all His ways, enjoyed His blessings, and still complained that He doesn't care for you?

Think about it for a minute. This isn't a game. It's life and death. If it's true and you blow it off, you just guaranteed yourself a spot in a land where you always thirst and never drink.

Go back to the beginning. Ask God to help you understand. He's offering the best party you've ever experienced. C'mon! Let's run into His house together.

Follow-up questions

1. Can you think of any other ways to enter God's presence? What are they?
2. Why do you think God gives such serious consequences for unbelief?
3. What do you think of when you hear the word "rest"? How good is God's rest?

Remembering How to Dance

Forget about your problems for a while.
Let a smile take over your lips and sing
To the universal King. Shout
'Til the atmosphere rings with your noise.
Rejoice, celebrate, DJ crack my soul with your beats.
MCs let your rhymin' get loud.
We're gonna let it rumble out,
Fill the air with the sound,
Gonna bring heaven downtown right where we live.

'Cause there's no greater King than the One that I sing to.
Move your new party shoes to the groove that is in you.
The fish in the sea know He lives in the deep,
And even trees wanna clap their hands.
Little lizards, they know how to dance.

'Cause there's no greater King than the One that I sing to.
Move your new party shoes to the groove that is in you.
The fish in the sea know He lives in the deep,
And even trees wanna clap their hands.
Little lizards they know how to dance.

Look around you.
His fingerprints rest in the delicate arch of flowers,
In the trickle of water, His refreshing voice.
Drink in the beauty of His love supporting each step,
Fall to knees cradled in the softness of Your maker.
The Everlasting One cares more deeply for you than all of His works.
And that's reason to party,
The best excuse to throw up your hands,
Give your hips some room to dance,
If you've been sitting too long then stand . . .

'Cause there's no greater King than the One that I sing to.
Move your new party shoes to the groove that is in you.
The fish in the sea know He lives in the deep,
And even trees wanna clap their hands.
Little lizards they know how to dance.

'Cause there's no greater King than the One that I sing to.
Move your new party shoes to the groove that is in you.
The fish in the sea know He lives in the deep,
And even trees wanna clap their hands.
Little lizards they know how to dance.

Open your ears to His voice today.
Let the Creator past your defenses.
Don't fight against God like those who escaped the bondage of
    Egypt.
They never believed that the miracles came from Him,
Never gave in to His love.
Though they walked through a sea turned dry,
Though the sky rained food,
Their pride wouldn't budge,
And their grudge dug a grave
In a wilderness where they couldn't find rest.
We don't have to be depressed,
Or resigned to their fate.
Let's celebrate, DJ crack my soul with your beats.
MCs let your rhymin' get loud.
We're gonna let it rumble out,
Fill the air with the sound,
Gonna bring heaven downtown right where we live.

'Cause there's no greater King than the One that I sing to.
Move your new party shoes to the groove that is in you.
The fish in the sea know He lives in the deep,

And even trees wanna clap their hands.
Little lizards they know how to dance.

'Cause there's no greater King than the One that I sing to.
Move your new party shoes to the groove that is in you.
The fish in the sea know He lives in the deep,
And even trees wanna clap their hands.
Little lizards they know how to dance.
Little children, don't forget how to dance.

A Goodness Punch in the Face – Psalm 20

You don't need to read this one twenty times to be moved by the opening lines: "When you're staring a nightmare of problems in the face, may it be the King of the universe that comes to your rescue."

See what I mean? Freaking *awesome*. Read it again. Let it sink in.

When *you're* staring a NIGHTMARE of problems in the face, may it be the KING OF THE UNIVERSE that comes to *your* rescue.

That's right. You.

Who knows why He takes time to care for helpless little you, for helpless little me. Who knows why He loves, but He does. He comes through. He's got the power to slay any dragon and the tenderness to soothe the most broken of hearts. Fix your hope on Him. He's your best chance for help.

The next line takes it further by saying "the name of the God of Jacob." It doesn't say the God of Israel, which is the name God gave Jacob *after* he had prevailed with God and men. He says "Jacob," aka deceiver, conniver, the guy who does things on his own and creates lots of problems for him and others. God's not the God of the perfect. He takes time to defend misfits who come to their senses and realize that they've gotten themselves into trouble. He sees your potential and calls you family when you're at your worst.

May the name of the God of Jacob send you help from the holy place.

The holy place, in Hebrew mentality housed the very heart of God's presence. He doesn't just call you to come to Him. He brings His heart, His desire, His holiness to you. He changes His location for your sake. And when the psalmist talks about "strengthening you out of Zion," that's the city where the King lives. It's Israel's home base. God's sanctuary and Zion stand next to each other. He unites His home with your home. Verse 2 essentially says, "May God live where you do."

You'll probably never fully understand what it means to bring the first produce of your field or your prized lamb to burn in the fire to God. I sure don't. But these would have been significant milestones in an Israelite's life. They gave "free-will offerings" just to honor God and declare that He's most important. It was like giving your favorite car to someone with no chance of getting it back. A lamb represented food, clothing, earning power. A bull represented about ten sheep. The bigger the offering, relative to your budget, the more it marked your heart as belonging to God.

So verse 3 says, "May God accept and keep in mind every good deed you've done." Burnt sacrifices would be payment for sin, the covering of past mistakes. So, "May God forget all your wrongs. May He see you as only good and only worthy of His love." Now think on everything you've read up to this point while the music plays (*Selah*).

Put verse 4 next to verse 1. God not only helps you when you're in the hole, He gives you everything your heart desires. And top that off with all your plans working out. He's not just going to come to your side and hold the enemy back. He wants you to live out your dreams, to succeed, to see the realization of your vision.

When that happens, everyone watching's going to celebrate. They'll revel in your rescue. The neighbors will see banners proclaiming the party is on. I don't know how we ended up equating holiness with quiet reverence. There's a place for that, sure, but you see a lot more shouting, laughing, dancing, and music, as opposed to quietness, in the Bible when people experience God's love. The cool thing is that with these lines corresponding to verse 2, the celebration happens when God's home gets united with yours. Want in on that? Want to have the King of the universe make your home His favorite hangout?

Personally I believe the last line of verse 5 corresponds with verse 3 and finishes the second section. It makes more sense to have it numbered as verse 6, although English translations don't separate it from verse 5. God fulfilling your petitions seems to fit pretty well with offerings and burnt sacrifices. Talk about an understatement. The psalm writer isn't just saying it again (like he would if he was a lame writer), he's throwing a sneaky punch to our brain to say, "That's the way God answers requests. He does better than you thought." There's no *Selah*, but this would be a good point for the music to play and let you contemplate that mind-blower, before the concluding section hits . . .

Now I know that God gives victory to His Messiah and those with Him.
He's not just going to acknowledge your trouble.
He'll swoop down from heaven with the power of His super-mega-galactic arsenal to save you.
Want to trust in a chariot that some man put together?
Or the power of a horse? (Or yourself?)
Fine. We're going to remember the character of Yahweh, our God who makes His home inside ours.
Other people bow down to themselves or their gods, and they fall.
We offer the good and bad of our past to the God who lives,
And He helps us stand with honor.

So . . . "Save, Lord!" he says as if throwing open his arms and flinging his head back to heaven. "I want You to rescue me every time I call, because you're so good!"

I agree. Don't you? Read it again if you don't. You've probably tried over and over to fix your own problems. I know I have. It always fails. When will you ever learn? If God's that good, you don't want anyone else to save you. Go to Him. Do it now. Drop your pride. Admit that you need His love. It doesn't matter what you've done in the past. He's got a party waiting. He wants to celebrate your return to His arms. He's desperate to display to the world how beautifully He made you.

May the King answer *you* with that much goodness every time you call.

Follow-up questions

1. When is it hardest for you to trust God to help you?
2. What's the biggest thing you've ever given to God?
3. How much of His goodness do you deserve?

God of Rescue

When the noose winds its coils round your neck,
When you've stretched 'cross the tracks of an onrushing train,
When pain cries your fear of the end,
You've got a Friend,
More real than the laws of physics,
Dedicated to being the God of misfits, traitors, deceivers, and even
    goody two-shoes.

He'll stick His neck in the path of that train,
Pull you from your noose,
Replace pain with peace,
Look fear straight in the face and laugh.
He remembers all the good of your past,
Swallows your shame in the flames of His love.
Let His music fill you up.

When gifts fit the secret dreams of your heart,
When you're avalanched by too much success,
We'll party to celebrate your happiness,
Raise our glasses,
Drown out the fireworks of heaven's joyous noise.
The King loves to get funky and rejoice.

His heart races to each whispered request,
Treads through murky blackness,
Cracks open the biggest can of holy whoop-ass might,
Forgetting the majesty and honor He deserves,
Offering Himself in place of His children.
You trust your weapons, schemes, and plans?
God breathes life to stars, and His mercy rescues forever.

You'll collapse under the burdens you choose,
But the King's offer is magic shoes,
Playground delight,
Bright eyes bursting with innocence,
Stillness drowning screams of your past,
An audience with the Maker of the universe,
His nearness bestowed the instant you dare to ask.

Because You *Don't* Deserve It – Psalm 51

David didn't deserve to write Psalm 51. He should have died for having sex with the wife of one of his most faithful servants, murdering him, and trying to cover it all up. Any one of those things required the death penalty. It's in the Law that God gave Moses.

But God didn't wipe him off the map; He sent Nathan, the prophet, with a story of a rich man who stole a poor farmer's only lamb instead of serving one of his own to feed a guest. David swore that the rich man should die for his evil, until Nathan said, "You're the man." Gulp.

What do you do when you're caught red-handed? Most of us run away. A few stand still and accept the bitter consequences of our actions. Hardly any of us have the audacity to look in the eyes of the One who's got power to end our life and ask for forgiveness and complete removal of all consequences. But that's what David does. I think it happened as he wrote this psalm. Put yourself in his shoes . . .

Imagine yourself kneeling. You grovel and sob because of how miserable you feel. Regret pierces your heart with images of what you've done. Seeing her naked beauty on the roof. Seducing Bathsheba. Looking at Uriah's face as he refused to sleep with his wife while his fellow soldiers endured the battlefield. The rage that possessed you. The moment you found out she was pregnant. Ordering Uriah's murder. The satisfaction when you found out he was dead. There's no escape. You deserve to die.

You start by appealing to the part of God's character that forgives.

> Give me mercy, because your love, kindness, and compassion overflow like no one else's.
> Erase my wrongdoing.
> Make me pure.
> Scrub me clean.
> Remember your tenderness most of all.

It seems like a long shot, but you keep going . . .

> I'm to blame. I did it all.

Your actions flash through your mind again.

> It's always there. I can't get rid of it. And I did it all to you.

Your plea for mercy isn't looking too good. Now I must confess that I don't totally understand when he says, "Against you and you only have I sinned." He clearly sinned against Bathsheba, Uriah, and the whole nation as well. God doesn't seem to gloss that over either, since he confronts David about it through Nathan the prophet and through consequences afterward. Plus, the phrase is connected to "that You may be found just when You speak and blameless when You judge" (NKJV).

I think David's telling God to judge Him like He did it all intentionally against Him. No matter how severe the sentence he receives, he trusts God's justice. It's the only thing I can think of that stays consistent with the rest of the story and God's character. Let's go with that. Now the next tricky verse . . .

> Look, I was born in iniquity and even conceived in sin . . .

I've heard speculation from people that David may have been his father's son but of a different mother than the rest of his brothers. Maybe that's why he got stuck watching sheep. Maybe that's why Jesse didn't bring him with the other brothers when Samuel came looking to anoint the next king. Whatever the background, it's pretty devastating to trace your own sin before your birth. You can't escape. It grips you everywhere.

You begin writing verse 6, repeating the same word as the previous verse for added emphasis (at least that's how it is in the original Hebrew). It's like you're screaming "Behold" or "Look," in an all-out attempt to win the compassion of God's heart . . .

> Look, maybe I was doomed from before birth,
> But You delight in finding what's hidden.
> You know me and make me to know Your wisdom.

As you finish the phrase, something happens inside. You realize that God can even go back before the start of sin and plant seeds of goodness. You start getting excited. You write the next two verses not as petitions, starting with a verb, but as declarations . . .

> You cleanse me on the outside, and I'm clean.
> You bathe me, and I'm purer than freshly fallen snow.
> You bring smiles, laughter, shouts of happiness to my ears,
> And everything that felt crushed starts to come alive.

Hope in God's forgiveness races to your fingers . . .

> Oh, please, don't look at all my wrongs.
> Wipe away even the unintentional mistakes.
> Don't just forgive me this time. Go all the way.
> Make a brand new heart for me, one that has no fault.
> Give me the right attitude.
> Whatever You do, don't throw me out of Your presence.

Let Your Spirit stay with me forever.

Give me the joy of being rescued by You and keep it fresh in my mind.

Can you feel the freshness of a clean conscience? Most of what we've heard in churches stops right there. But you don't. You're bursting with joy. You want more than just to be right, to be even on the sin scale . . .

I'm gonna teach other lawbreakers how merciful you are, God.

They'll come running back to you.

Wipe away the guilt of the blood I've shed,

And no one will be able to shut my singing down.

Everyone will hear melodies of Your saving power, Your holiness.

My lips will make You famous.

Because You don't want gifts, more punishment, or I'd throw myself on the altar.

You care about the hurt of my heart, genuine humility.

That's what You want.

Humility and awe sweep you out into God's heart. Now that your eyes have locked back onto Him, you start seeing the whole situation from His perspective. For the first time since your sin, your heart bursts with His desire for the people who look to you for leadership.

Don't stop with me. Be good to Your people.

Build our boundaries back up.

Then we won't be giving offerings out of trying to get right.

They'll ascend from clean consciences, joyful desires to honor You.

You'll get the worship that You deserve.

The world will know what a merciful and glorious God You are.

Incredible. Even the structure displays it. Verses 1–8 parallel verses 9–17. First David authentically repents and receives cleansing. Then he asks for restoration and becomes an evangelist and worshiper.

Finally, he caps it off in verses 18 and 19 with his request for the blessing of Israel and a national heart dedicated to the honor that God deserves.

Just thinking through it helps you see the transformation. Writing it changes you even more. David went from selfish leader, deceiver, adulterer, and murderer, to king with a clean heart, willing to lay down his life for his people. That's what the real God does when you pour out your sin on His lap.

If only everyone ran to God when they sinned, instead of away from Him. He loves giving His heart to those who don't deserve it. He wants to make your rescue His excuse to show the world just how much He loves. How much will you let Him rescue you?

Follow-up questions

1. When you mess up where do you usually go, or what do you do that makes you feel better?
2. Is there a person in your life that you can run to for forgiveness, healing, etc.? Who?
3. What do you think would happen if you started telling everyone about how your failures have been forgiven?

Getting Better Than What I Deserve

Please, be merciful to me.
I don't deserve Your love.
I don't deserve Your kindness, forgiveness,
My hands bear the stain of the violence and blood
That I can't wash away,
Can't scrub my heart clean.
No penance could quiet this raging, dark sea.
Please, pour out all Your mercy on me,
Just because it's who You are.

Don't blame anyone else.
I see sin everywhere I look.
It drips from each page of my life,
And nothing excuses how I hurled all my hatred at You.
Every sentence You've spoken strikes true.
Even in Your justice
Still You sparkle like morning dew.

From the beginning I came out flawed, bent, and twisted,
Formed in shame from an act of sin.
But deep within You're still searching for truth,
Rewriting my past long before I was formed,
Like snow newborn white,
Bathed in squeaky clean delight.
You flood my life with songs and laughter,
Turning the sting of discipline into innocent glee.

Don't let Your eyes see.
Make every one of my failures disappear.
Keep me snuggled near to Your chest.
Fashion a new, living skin.
I'll trade my broken one in

For a clean conscience,
A smile-to-the-rooftops funky dance,
A let's-get-it-on, I'm ready 'cause You're with me attitude.
I can teach other lawbreakers Your goodness,
'Cause I've tasted the feast of Your gourmet food.
And they return to Your arms to become a child like You've made
    me.

Set me free from bloodshed, please, my God,
You're the only God who could save me.
I'm dripping melodies of Your righteousness,
Shouting out the biggest celebration from these open lips.
If You wanted me to give up my most prized possession, I would
    give it,
But You couldn't care less about gifts.
You're after my heart,
Open, vulnerable, fully exposed to Your love.
You never reject my shattered spirit.

Rebuild the fortress of Your protection.
Set these ruined walls into wholeness and restored health
So I can give out of my overflow,
Time and delight and creativity that only grows,
Pouring out all the honor and worship that You deserve.

What If God Doesn't Answer? – Psalm 88

Imagine yourself locked in a small, dirty room. Rope shackles your hands and feet to a chair. One light flickers, dangling just above your head. Beads of sweat tickle your forehead from the heat of the bulb. You can't scratch the itch. Heavy breathing and threats pummel your ears. Every voice is foreign and full of hate. Each word threatens your life. "You're about to wish you'd never been born." Blows begin punishing your face and body, splitting your skin. One of your ribs splinters. Each breath stabs pain. No escape. You're dead with a heartbeat. And you have no clue what you did wrong.

What name do you call to rescue you in that moment? What if He doesn't answer?

Psalm 88 never gives a solution to its questions. If anything it stirs them up, pointing a finger at God, questioning His faithfulness and love. It seems like blasphemy. Yet it stands in the Bible. God didn't snuff out Heman the Ezrahite before he finished writing it. Israel sang it with a flute accompaniment as part of their worship. Put yourself in their shoes. Join with them. Ask God and expect Him to respond . . .

Oh, Yahweh, God of my rescue, I cry day and night to You.
Let my prayer reach Your face. Stretch Your ear to my cry.
For my soul is weary of problems. My life touches the underworld.

I'm counted with those who descend to the grave. I've become a warrior with no strength.

Mixed with the dead, like a victim lying in a tomb, severed from Your power and memory.

You've plunged me to the deepest dark pit of the netherworld, in shadows.

You've spent Your rage on me and held me under the crashing waves.

A cascade of flute pours complaints over you. Your own problems tower higher. It feels like God Himself has His hand on your head, forcing you under the water where the monsters of the deep tear and rip your flesh. Why do you have to suffer? Where's God? It's His character to save, to rescue. Where is He? When will He finally answer? Will He send anyone to help? Now it gets more desperate . . .

You've taken my friends away and made me disgusting to them in a prison I can't escape.

I waste away in humiliation even though I've called You, Yahweh, and humbled myself before You.

Will you do miracles for the dead? Will ghosts stand and speak their praise of You?!

The flutes play frenetically. Strings mix their anger with yours. Your emotions ache. You feel the isolation, the shame. It doesn't seem to matter how much you pray. You can't perform enough religious rituals to make things better. Analyzing your situation with logic only makes you angrier and more desperate for justice. You long for the intensity to ratchet down just a bit. Maybe resolution will show up. But then it kicks into a higher gear . . .

Will Your mercy matter in my tomb . . . Your kindness and faithfulness when I'm destroyed?

Will You show Your miracles in darkness, or your justice in the land where all is forgotten?

I've shouted to You for help, Yahweh, and at the break of day my prayer confronts You.

Yahweh, why do You reject my soul? Why do you hide Your face from me?

I don't understand why I've been poor and ready to die since childhood, carrying a dread of You.

Your anger floods me. Your terrors annihilate me.

They swirl around me like water every day. They surround me completely.

You've removed lover, friends, and anyone who knows me. Darkness.

Everything stops. No music. No words. You wait. You hear nothing.

Read the psalm again. Feel the anger, the rejection, the despair, the loneliness poke and scratch your insides. This is as real as it gets. It's anything but comfortable.

Despite the lack of hope, Heman keeps coming back to God, pointing his finger, accusing God with His own covenant. No other god claims to be as just and faithful. No other god even claims to care about humans. But Yahweh has. Heman won't let Yahweh forget His promises. He's not going somewhere else to get his needs met. Even if he ends up in total darkness, he's waiting for God to save him.

"You promised, God!" "Where *were* you when their laughter shoved and humiliated me in a corner?" "How could you let him abuse me like that?" "Why did my daughter have to feel their dirty hands grope and probe her again and again?" "I was powerless." "None of my friends or acquaintances or loved ones could do anything to help."

Heman's pointing out that in those gut-wrenching moments, it's God who's going to rescue, or nothing at all.

You've probably never experienced the kind of hardships that physically tortured Dietrich Bonhoeffer's, Brother Yun's, or any martyr's mind and body. Then again, maybe you have. Whatever your situation, you've felt the blows of life pummel your heart. You've wrestled with doubt. Have you ever felt like giving up? Does God really care when you suffer? When death's at your door, are you still going to cling to Yahweh? Will He save you? If you die with no relief from the daily terrors, humiliation, and agony, will you still put your trust in Him?

This isn't a game. He's listening and real. Ask Him your toughest questions, even if they sound blasphemous. Pour out all your fury. Expose your darkest secrets. Let the injustice you've suffered pound on His chest. Tell Him how your father beat you. Whisper the name of the one who stole your innocence. Empty the shame. Vent all your rage. Let the tears flow like rivers. Sob and shake with the pain right in His lap. He wants to know. He's here. You'll never break His love. You can't shock Him with your depravity. Even your cursing won't scare Him away.

The God who rescues can take it. Are you willing to expose your heart to Him?

Follow-up questions

1. What's the worst thing you've ever said to (or thought about) God? (God already knows, so you're safe to share it.)
2. How often do you wrestle with doubt about God being real or loving you?
3. Which person in your life would never betray you? How do you know?

The God Who Saves Me?

Oh, Lord, the God who saves me day and night, day and night.
Oh, Lord, the God who saves me day and night, day and night.

My prayer stretches to reach You,
To feel the kiss of Your gaze, turn Your ears my way,
Send me a beacon of hope,
Because I'm sinking, drowning, swallowing, groping,
The grave's laughing grin,
My chest caving in.
I've got no will to fight this closing crypt,
Skin shredded and torn, voiceless as the stillborn,
Thrown beneath a pit of no hope,
An ocean pressing, crushing, gnawing, rusting,
Ripping spirits out of Your grip.
Reality slips
And flips the switch of darkness where even God can't see.
It's me the shadow, severed from the light,
Filled with all Your fury, punished as the tide breaks,
Groaning 'cause these bones ache,
Lying with the buried dead, stifled screaming!

Oh, Lord, the God who saves me day and night, day and night.
Oh, Lord, the God who saves me day and night, day and night.
Oh, Lord, the God who saves me day and night, day and night.
Oh, Lord, the God who saves me day and night, day and night.

All my friends shudder with the memory of my face,
Locked beneath the waves,
Reaching far away,
Fading from the day,
Yahweh, it's You that I wrestle to pull near,
My hands plead, but You're farther than the stars.

Lonely tears, a single bed,
Can the grave sing You its songs?

Will Your wonders be shown to the dead?
Does Your mercy extend to my final breath?
Can You reach to the depths of the sea?
'Cause I'm drowning, drowning!

Oh, Lord, the God who saves me day and night, day and night.
Oh, Lord, the God who saves me day and night, day and night.
Oh, Lord, the God who saves me day and night, day and night.
Oh, Lord, the God who saves me day and night, day and night.

Does hell tell of all Your love and kindness?
Are shattered dreams Your seal of faithfulness?
The end of all Your miracles?
Swallowed like an ant into the acid of oblivion?
I pounded till my fists bled raw,
Poured out my heart through an open jaw.
How do You let me drown?
You see me sinking down,
And it's been this way since I was a boy.
Your terror leaves me annoyed.
It washes over me, cuts me, leaves me broken,
All around, crashing sounds, tying me with fever,
Lovers, friends and all who cared for me, fading into memory,
Nothingness.

Oh, Lord, the God who saves me day and night, day and night.
Oh, Lord, the God who saves me . . .

125

You Want Your Filth? Or Something Better? – Psalm 132

Can you remember the filthy swamp of misfortune and bad decisions that David endured? Especially after he was anointed to be king? Sure he won tons of battles. Yes, he was rich and feared. Then he committed adultery and murdered one of his mighty men. His oldest son, Amnon, raped Absalom's, his third son's, daughter. Then Absalom murdered Amnon and tried to kill David and steal the kingdom. And that's just his own family. Murders and treachery riddled his most trusted advisors. His reign was rocky at best.

Despite all that, he clung to the Lord as being the One who had blessed him, not the one who had caused the problems. "I'm going to make Him famous," David swore. "I'm going to make sure that God has a permanent place to live in our land. God's going to get the honor that He deserves from us, no matter what it takes me."

So to remind God, and more importantly, Israel, of David's vow, the psalmist(s) composed this song of ascents. It's meant to be sung on the way up Zion, the holy mountain where God made His home. With each step toward the top you're supposed to sing a line. The writer(s) conspicuously use the name Jacob again, instead of Israel. "If you made amazing promises to that screwed up guy, you can bless us, too." Now look at David's oath:

I won't go into my room.
I won't get into bed.
I won't let my eyes know sleep.
I won't let my eyelids droop
Until I find a place for God,
A place where He will live.

Combine that with music that goes up and up, and David's desire culminates at God living with Him. Could a human have any better intention? So now the people have to respond to that, and the music returns to the beginning melody to build with it:

We heard about it in Ephrathah
We found it in the fields of Jaar
Let's go to His tabernacle
Let's humble ourselves at His feet
Come to Your resting place!
Come with all of Your strength!
Clothe Your priests with spotlessness
Make us erupt with shouts of joy!

Look a little closer at the word "Ephrathah." Another name for it is Bethlehem, David's (and some other famous guy's) little home-town in the tribe of Judah. It means "place of fruitfulness" and is near Bethel, where Rachel, Jacob's second wife and the mother of Joseph and Benjamin, died and was buried. It's also a region in the tribe of Ephraim, where the Ark of the Covenant was lost to the Philistines.

Which of these four images did it generate in their minds? All of them. The people are saying, "We heard about God in our humble beginnings, our sorrow, our loss. He's going to make us fruitful."

Do you know what they found in the fields of Jaar? Here's a paraphrase of the story from 1 Samuel 4–7. The Philistines had oppressed and invaded Israel for several generations, and they came looking for blood again. Israel took the Ark of the Covenant out into battle thinking that its magic power would help them win. Instead, the Philistines fought harder, won the battle, and captured the Ark. Israel lost its high priest, his sons, and the symbol of God's presence with them in one day. Shiloh, the location of the tabernacle, lay destroyed and forgotten forever thereafter.

Things didn't go so well for the Philistines either. Their chief god, Dagon, fell face first toward the Ark. Tumors and plagues ravaged their cities. They figured that the God of Israel must be sending them an angry message. So they put the Ark in a cart with no driver and watched as the cows pulled it straight to Israel. It stopped in the fields surrounding Kirjath Jearim, or the fields of Jaar. It stayed there for 20–60 years, waiting for Israel to make a home for it. Jaar also literally means forest, or wood. So the fields of Jaar would evoke images of a meadow, where animals come to feed.

Israel had learned a hard lesson. Holy objects and rituals don't guarantee God's presence. They wanted God to make His home with them, to cover them in His goodness so they could celebrate loudly.

Now that you know a little something about "Ephrathah," look at verse 10, a natural place for the music to return to the very beginning. The repetition of "David" should trigger your brain to remember his affliction and vow.

Don't let the Messiah miss us, for David's sake.
No matter what, Yahweh won't change His mind. I'm going to make your sons to rule. If they stay true to My covenant and follow My direction, they'll rule forever.

God keeps going, upping the ante, indicating that He started it in the first place . . .

Yahweh Himself chose Zion. He wants it as His permanent residence.
I'm going to live here forever. This is where I'll live, because I desired it.
I'll pour out so much fruitfulness, even the poor will have full bellies.
I'll make your priests agents of rescue. You'll shout so that it shakes the earth.

Right about now, the music's kicking, and God hasn't just answered everything the people asked for. He's promised better than they wanted. Now comes the bridge and something they'd never considered . . .

> I'm going to make David's horn grow. I'll prepare a lamp for the Messiah.

You probably haven't heard anyone tell you, "Man, your horn is growing like crazy!" or "His horn sure has grown these past few years." John Gill's *Exposition of the Bible* says that in the time that this was written, the term "horn" applied to the power and might of kings, like the horns of a bull that push things out of their way the bigger and stronger they get.

When you see that phrase "prepare the lamp" the clearest image you'd probably get is that you're the lamp, the physical housing, while the Messiah is the light. God's going to fashion you into something worthy and capable of containing and beaming the power of His goodness to the world. Pretty mind-blowing. But I think there's more to it.

The other place in Jewish culture where people prepare lamps is before weddings. Remember the parable of the wise and foolish virgins? The bride would prepare and beautify herself while the groom built them a home. Her duty was to keep her lamp burning brightly, to be ready to go with him to their new home when he came.

So, as the music soars to new heights at the end of the psalm, God says,

> I'm going to make you truly glorious so that you become a people ready to marry Me, to have My life and love burning in you forever.

That's what God's really like. You ask Him to make His home in you; He changes you into more incredible people than you hoped. Then you share in His glory forever! Whoa! Chills. But that's still not the end.

129

The Messiah's enemies will be forgotten and covered in shame. But His kingdom, His power, splendor, and prosperity will grow, spread and bloom like a garden that continues to fill the earth with its beauty.

The word usually translated as "shine" has a double meaning of light (connecting to the lamp picture) and blossoming plants (connecting to what we lost in Eden). They only requested God to remember their troubles and come live with them. He promised to make them His forever home and more beautiful than they'd ever imagined, so they could marry His Son. Together, they would live in a kingdom that grows, blossoms, and floods the earth with light. Who could refuse a reward like that?

The nation of Israel didn't take God up on His offer. They chose other gods, and then later, the rules, over His presence. But the offer's still open. God wants to turn your problems and discomforts into beauty. He wants you to be part of the glorious bride. He's offering to make you worthy to marry His Son. Will you say yes?

Follow-up questions

1. Which of your religious rituals (examples: going to church, singing "worship" songs, praying at meal times, etc.) do you think God cares about least?
2. How would your life change if the God of the universe moved into your room with you?
3. How many times do you have to turn God down in order to get the everlasting shame reserved for the "wicked"?

Bitter and Sweet

Bitter and sweet.
Bitter and sweet when defeat whispers hope in reply.
All the trying and struggle, the shipwreck and trouble,
If breezes don't swell these sails,
We'll leap from the rails,
Kick our feet through the waves,
Blistered hands on the oars,
'til Your toes caress our sandy shores.
Drop Your anchor in our chests.
Dismantle Your ship and build a home in these hearts,
Your children,
Sweet sharing,
The bliss,
Our journey.

We lost You in the bitterness of planes toppling twin towers,
Souls drowning under tsunami seas,
Rituals crashing on wreckage,
Security dying under waves,
But You glided Your ship through dust and debris,
Revealed kindness through courage of strangers,
Outpourings of relief from across the world.
We saw You in their eyes.
Cries for relief became comfort and rest,
And we want to give our best,
Shout with all the joy in our breath to a King who tears His robe to
    bandage wounds.
Wrap our hearts in all Your goodness.
Make us forget all our loss in the music of joy.

Bitter and sweet.
Bitter and sweet when our past forgets pain in a promise.

For the sake of Your beloved, don't leave us to save ourselves.
"The sun might forget how to shine.
The tides might go still.
Earth may spin to a stop.
A mother might abandon her newborn child,
But I'll never regret My promise to you.
I'm coming, a Savior to reshape the earth.
Even if you reject Me, I'll still see your worth.
I choose you, a treasure, the firstborn, My home,
Your beggars, My princes, your birthright a place by My throne.

"Lose your bitterness in the joining of our desire.
Be the aid workers rushing toward a catastrophe,
Soldiers fighting to rescue a drowning child,
A harbor of refuge . . . and celebration,
Sweetness that heals . . . and indulges,
Your goodness sparkling across seas,
Awakening hope for just a glimpse
Of your wedding dress,
More than the best you've dreamed."

We're the bride of a King so radiantly kind,
His enemies forget how to fight.
They kneel in awe,
The sun feels small when it stares at the brightness of His face.
Come take Your place in our hearts, oh, God!
Make us lost in Your music of joy.

When Betrayal Murders Joy – Psalm 42 and 43

Your son has betrayed you. Not like taken the keys to your car or talked behind your back betrayed you. He's strategically manipulated your friends and family for years until most of them prefer him. You've lost respect, your wealth, and your home. Now he wants to kill you.

You, your family, and the only friends who won't desert you flee for your lives. You cross the wilderness east of Jerusalem on foot, using up all your water supply. Everyone's mouth yearns for water. Licking your lips, the salt from your sweat only makes you thirstier. Pretty soon you begin to see evidence of moisture. Desert flowers, a tiny tree, scattered grass begin to spring up. Suddenly a valley stretches down in front of you, and all you see is green.

You descend, thinking of the baths you used to take at home. But there's very little water at this time of year in the Jordan. You plod on, hoping you'll make it.

As you go north, old friends meet you with water and food. Thank God. Who knows if the kids could have made it another thirty miles until the Sea of Chinnereth. Once everyone feels a bit refreshed, you get going again. After another twenty minutes of walking, an old man starts yelling at you from the other side of the valley.

"Get out! Keep going, you murderous, thief of the throne. You stole it from our family. You killed us all! God's paying you back through your son. Where's He now? How ya gonna sing to God now?

No tabernacle. None of your pagan choirs. You're caught in the trap of your own evil. You dog! You liar! You bloodthirsty whore!"

Mile after mile he screams. You remember how many times Saul tried to kill you, how many times you could have killed him and didn't. Though it's sucking the life out of everyone with you, you keep walking, refusing to let Abishai "take care of him."

"I didn't kill Saul then, and I'm not killing his family now. Let him curse, Abishai."

"But he lies. I was with you all those years running from Saul!"

"And did I ever once think of hurting any of his family?"

"No, my king." Abishai drops his head in shame. "Me and my brothers . . . we were the ones . . ."

You plod on through the heat and the memories. You thought you'd never be a refugee again. You thought God would make your kingdom last forever. Now it's all coming to an end.

In a few more miles, the trickle of the Jordan whispers in your ears. You must be getting close to the Sea of Galilee. Mount Hermon beckons from its snow-capped peaks.

"That's where we're going, Solomon," you say to your little boy walking beside you.

"Are we gonna have to walk?"

"No, son, I'll carry you."

Twenty more miles to Mizar, the hill south of Hermon where waterfalls drown out sound and deer graze with no fear. You'll have enough food if you make it. Hopefully the Phoenicians and Syrians won't kill you. What you wouldn't give to hear the sounds of Zion again. If only you could go back to the day when you led the whole nation in bringing the Ark back. The dancing. The feasting. God's pleasure . . .

❋   ❋   ❋

Six months pass since Absalom's reign has ended. You won. The throne is yours again. But home doesn't feel like home anymore. Every few hours you still gaze longingly out the window toward the tree where Absalom hung, and Joab . . . If only you . . .

"My king!" Abishai stands at the door. At least it's not Joab. "The sons of Korah are here, sire . . . with . . . the song."

"I'll come to them."

"Yes, sire."

Abishai kneels, his eyes glued to the floor. As you pass, you pause and touch his head. He catches your eyes, sees the sorrow and drops his head again. "I wish . . . If only I could have stopped . . ."

"Don't say it. I know."

You trudge to the receiving room. They stand, solemn and excited, dripping with the aura of worship, like always. Shallum blurts out before you sit down, "We . . . we finished it, sire. It . . . it . . . it came during last week's evening . . . uh . . . prayers. Not one person left without tears . . . and hope. We've been . . . been singing and refining it all week. We . . . we . . . we . . ."

"We wanted to make sure it fit, your majesty," Heman says, helping Shallum out.

Shallum continues. "Right. It fits. It really fits. So cool. So really cool. It . . . it . . . it's in two parts. But there . . . there's an unexpected . . ."

"Well sing it for me. Teach it to me. It's the best . . ." you struggle, but keep it together . . . "the best news I've had . . . since . . ."

"We know, sire," Heman says, looking straight in your eyes with compassion. "Guys . . ."

The harps begin strumming, no, flowing into your ears. One of the smallest ones lets out a shimmer of notes. The sons of Korah interweave deep, harmonic humming. You remember how greedily everyone drank when you arrived in Mizar, how your soul ached . . . how it still aches. Then Shallum sings out . . .

As the deer pants for streams of water, so my soul pants for You, God.
My soul thirsts for God, for the flowing God. When will I come and see
God's presence?

My tears are my bread day and night, while they say all day, "Where is your God?"
I remember these and pour them on my soul.

I used to pass through the crowds and walk in procession to God's house,
With joyful shouting and songs of thanks, a roar of celebrating and feasting.

Why are you bowed down, my soul? Why are you churning inside me?
Be confident in God, for I will again speak my praise to Him for the salvation of His face.

You remember how you carried Solomon, how he fell asleep in your arms. God's heartbeat pulses through your body as the drums keep time. Before and behind you loomed sorrow, but you felt God's power pulling you toward water, toward safety, toward refreshing.
The original melody returns, but fuller, deeper, more intense. You expect to hear Shallum's voice, but Heman's pierces the air . . .

God, my soul is bowed down on me,
So I remember You from the Jordan, Mt. Hermon and Mt. Mizar.

Abyss cries to abyss at the roar of Your rushing torrents.
All Your breakers and billows have passed through me.

Yahweh will command His kindness by day,
And in the night, His song, my song from Him as a prayer to God for my life.

I will say to God my fortress, "Why have You ignored me?
Why do I mourn in darkness from the pressure of my enemy?"

In shattering my limbs these adversaries taunt me,
While they say all day, "Where is your God?"

Why are you bowed down, my soul? Why are you churning inside me?
Be confident in God, for I will again speak my praise to Him for the
salvation of my face and because He's my God.

The music rushes you away with your tears. God's sorrow catches you
in His arms, and you know He knows. Comfort fills your heart as you
let it go. The musicians return to the original melody one more time,
now majestic and full . . .

Judge me, God, and dispute my dispute against an ungodly nation.
Deliver me from the treacherous and perverse man.

For You're my stronghold, God. Why have You abandoned me?
Why do I mourn in darkness from the pressure of my enemy?

Send out Your light and truth. Let them guide me.
Let them bring me to Your holy mountain, to Your home.

And I'll go to the altar of God, to the God of my delight and gladness
And I'll *yadah* You on my harp, God, my God.

Why are you bowed down, my soul? Why are you churning inside
me?
Be confident in God, for I will again speak my praise to Him for the
salvation of my face and because He's my God.

"Was it . . . ?" Heman asks.

"Perfect . . . Thank you. I love the repeats and twists and how you
saved the answer for the very end."

"We didn't want it to be perfectly happy in your circumstances.
Your life . . . er . . . uh . . . our lives aren't like that."

"And that's why you wrote His song, my song, and the face of Him,
face of me."

"Absolutely, my king."

"I still can't get over how the second verse ends with that taunting that Shimei screamed at me . . ."

"The 'where is your God?' part?"

"Yeah, and how at the very last you answered it with, 'God . . . my God,' and your voice . . . where'd you learn to sing like that?"

"Shallum coached me, but, I don't know, it just poured out."

"Sounds like Yahweh. Want to pour it out again?"

The sons of Korah never need to be asked twice to sing. They start it up. You join in. You all sing it again and again, mixing in new verses for the rest of the day. Everyone in the palace sighs a bit of relief. The king has finally returned, the one they fell in love with so many years ago. Soon they're all humming their new favorite. In a few hundred years, Jonah will reference your words (Jonah 2:3) as he writes about life inside a whale. For now, you just enjoy a delicious bath in the music of God's comfort.

Late that night you look out your bedroom window. Calm has returned to Israel. But you feel something greater stirring. A deep hope grows for the son who loves sleeping in your arms. Somehow out of sorrow springs comfort. Into the depths of betrayal, the ancient oceans of chaos, God poured His refreshing. Everywhere you go His home moves with you. Could you ever make something so glorious that the world would know how beautiful He is to stay faithful to a basket case like you?

Two psalms or one?

Look carefully at Psalm 42 and 43. They read so well if you read them straight through. Psalm 43 seems to continue and complete the building theme of Psalm 42, even culminating in the same repeated refrain at the end. Notice how the ideas of "rejoicing on the way to the house of God" (first stanza) and "mourning in darkness from the pressure of my enemy" (second stanza) both appear in Psalm 43 with a resolution? From a writer's perspective, that ain't no coincidence.

Is it all just made up? Well . . .

In my research I discovered that quite a few scholars believe them to be part of the same psalm. It's not just the similar style and continuing theme. Psalm 43 doesn't have a title, while all the psalms around it do. It's grouped with other works of the sons of Korah. Don't worry, that's not adding or subtracting from the Bible. It's just a slight variation in the translation from Hebrew to English.

Follow-up questions

1. How long does it take to get over the death of someone you love? What about the death of one of your dreams?
2. How do you usually respond when someone hurts your feelings?
3. What happens if you shove it down and try to avoid the hurt inside you?

Deep-sea Creature

Deep calls unto Deep.
I weep on the steep banks of a ravine,
Overlooking the scene of a surging, torrent waterfall
Beating on drums in my ears.
Globs of tears flow from the churning ointment in my chest.
People surround the glass shores of its pools,
Reposing in the sun,
Dipping chubby toes in pure waters,
Wading to their ankles with plodding feet,
Soak like a bath of Epsom salt,
A hypnotically somnambulant picture of life.

The surface is still, but my passion kills complacency.
I am thirsty, weary, bursting nearly to the threshold of solid, gas,
    and liquid interface,
Collision of three worlds . . .
Firm, impenetrable, and supporting.
Weightless vapor, tasteless, thin, light, and unable to be grasped.
Flowing, slippery soft clothing, cool, wet, and refreshing,
I am drinking in the third world of matter,
Falling on my knees as face meets pleasing draughts,
Laughter bubbling, washing my briared throat,
Filling the moat around my heart castle
As deep calls unto Deep.

Asleep to the heap of curious, fat stares
Gazing from comfortable chairs on my thin, lithe body.
Beating of drums from my inner kingdom
Yearns for more water,
Hotter the Potter's hands on tottering clay.
Who cares what they say!
I rush to the fray and leap, for a moment suspended in flight until . . .

Plunging like a released arrow into the heart of the pool,
Piercing into depths.
My breath is failing,
Expiring as sweet moisture presses in my flaring nostrils.
My eyes are wide with terror . . . and joy,
Open to this new universe of wonder.
Legs kick, arms flail, straight for the boiling center.
The pounding pulse from above,
Love from the heavens pins me on the bottom,
Purging hard billows urging release of my densely layered onion.
I am undone!
Blunt hammers, tenderizing clamor on my soul.
I want the whole deal!
Peel me open, water.
Gush into my castle walls.
Fall my vulnerability to Your delight.
I cannot be content tonight under thin sheets of rest
Returning from this blessed place,
Pulse racing through dream mountains
As deep calls unto Deep.

Creeping to peep out my window glass,
Floating the walls I pass through matter boundaries that held me
    before,
Soaring into liquid skies,
My disguise is gone.
Fly under Your love-waterfall,
Pounding, resounding my resonant frequency.
Decency is lost in sea waves.
Unreason waves goodbye to standard days.
I cannot stay away, pray, play, lay to rest my hunger,
Growing younger, more childlike and eager.
Grow the size of Your faucet!
Pour the star brightness!

Cause it to fill my receptacle,

A spectacle of transformation into a deep-sea creature.

Reach your unmeasured, pressured heights and length and width
and depths.

You are heaving in my chest.

Walls of my heart have fallen, ruins.

I am Your meadow.

Run through me.

You are free without gates.

Every locked place is open.

Delve in this swamp.

Stagnant water become a fresh spring fountain that swirls and
furls

Beating streams redeemed and united with your heart's cry,

As deep calls unto Deep.

The Harshest of Men – Psalm 36

"Sire!"

"Abishai, you came. I'm sorry it's so late."

"Did one of Sheba's men start another rebellion?"

"No, I . . ."

"Is it the Edomites?"

"No, it's . . ."

"Whatever you need, my king."

"Are you gonna let me finish?"

"Sorry, sire," he says and bows low.

"Get up. This isn't king stuff. And it's 2a.m. Really, I'm sorry."

"I'm happy to serve you at any time. You know that, your majesty."

"Come sit with me."

"Sire?"

"I just wrote a song."

"Want me to get the sons of . . . ?"

"No. I need *you*."

"But my mind's only good with weapons and tactics and killing and . . ."

"I don't need your *help* with the song."

"Thank God. Then why . . . ?"

"The Spirit came on me as I was going to sleep. I had to write it down. The voice of evil began speaking to me, and then Yahweh started showing me pictures of His love and kindness. I thought it was just about Ahithophel. And it was. But then it made me think about your brother."

"Asahel? But he's slept with our father for years. And maybe he was rash, but he wasn't . . ."

"Not Asahel, Joab."

"Joab?"

"You know what I mean. Three times now . . ."

"Please. Don't make me kill my brother. You know I'd journey with you to the underworld, but don't . . ."

"I don't want you to kill anyone, Abishai. Relax! Why do you Zeruiah boys always think of death as the first option?"

At the mention of his father Abishai drops his head, unable to speak. You wish you could help.

"What did he do to your family that wrapped thorns of rage so tightly round your heart? And Joab's?" you ask.

"He . . . I . . . We never . . . Sire, I'm sorry . . . I just . . . I just can't . . . I just can't find the words."

You've never seen Abishai show any emotion but ferocity. Now he's a little boy, watching some horror he can never tell. "You don't have to say, my friend. You're safe. I wish I could help you go back and undo whatever . . ."

"You've already done more than any other man would," he says, flinging the tear off his hand. "It's why any of us would give our life . . ."

"I don't deserve the honor. My past is littered with my own wrong . . . and God's forgiveness. It's why I'm so concerned for Joab. It's not just Absalom's death. He keeps choosing Ahithophel's path."

"I know. I try to talk to him, but he doesn't listen. He keeps saying, 'The ground cries out for blood. Moses gave us cities of refuge, and if the killer of a family member doesn't get there, God gives me the right to avenge.' He uses the Torah to justify everything he's done. He never says he's sorry anymore. He says he has a completely clean conscience. He doesn't even feel it."

"He's told me he never regretted a thing about how he killed Abner," you offer. "I haven't spoken to him about . . ." You drop your head as the sting of Absalom's death hits your still recovering heart.

"Don't. He's not . . . You won't . . . want to . . . hear."

"It's okay. You don't have to worry about me doing something to Joab."

"But he's killed Amasa now, and . . . your . . ."

"But taking his life won't bring back Absalom or anyone else. It only stains more blood on us all. I think it's what Yahweh was trying to show me with this song."

"Then let me hear, my king. You know music doesn't touch me . . . like it does you. But, I'll listen."

"All right then." You pray under your breath before you begin. "Yahweh, sing through what You've helped me write." You begin strumming your little harp. The notes tiptoe through the room. Once the melody is set, you strike the body of the harp with your thumbnail, and begin to sing . . .

Sin makes a prophetic declaration to the criminal deep within my heart.
His eyes see no awe of God.

For he chooses to believe what he wants to when he sees
Until he discovers depravity, until he hates.

His mouth speaks trouble and treachery.
He's lost the ability to understand and do good.

He imagines trouble when he lies down.
He takes his stand on a road that's not good.
He doesn't refuse evil.

Your heart pours out for your friend. "Please, Yahweh, don't let him destroy himself," you think, as the notes grow louder. You notice Abishai, holding his face in his hands. "Please let this bring healing to Abishai's heart, too."

As you begin thinking on Yahweh's goodness, you play softer, more soothing melodies. You imagine Joab's heart melting as each image leaps out through the lyrics . . .

Yahweh, the sky displays your kindness.
Your faithfulness reaches the clouds.

Your justice is like the divine mountains.
Your judgments like the vast abyss.
You deliver man and beast.

How costly is Your kindness, O God,
And children flee for protection under the shade of Your wing.

They intoxicate themselves from the bounty of Your house,
And you intoxicate them with the torrent of your luxuries.

For in You is the spring of life.
In Your light we see light.

You get carried away on the harp. Liquid love attacks you and Abishai. You attempt to keep playing, but the notes don't matter. Pretty soon you're both lying on the floor, face up, overcome by Yahweh's presence. His compassion and mercy consume every thought. And then you remember Joab, and the rest of the song. So you mix the melody from both verses. All your intensity spills over as you sing. You almost stop playing in shock as Abishai starts repeating each line with his tone-deaf voice.

Stretch out Your kindness to those who know You intimately . . .
Stretch out Your kindness to those who know You intimately . . .

And Your justice to the heart that stands in integrity.
And Your justice to the heart that stands in integrity.

Don't let a prideful attitude enter me,
Don't let a prideful attitude enter me,

And don't let me wander in the strength of criminals.
And don't let me wander in the strength of criminals.

That's where those who make trouble have fallen.

Abishai stops singing, but you continue.

"They've been thrown down and can't find the strength to stand."

Your fingers stop. "You sang! Why'd you . . . ?" but Abishai cuts you off.

"Please, Yahweh, don't let Joab go down that road. Turn him around. Let him see how he's twisted your goodness to justify such evil. Don't let him fall like Ahithophel. Save his family! Protect his children. Don't let them follow in the footsteps of their father!"

Abishai's compassion provokes your own heart. "Please, Yahweh, for my friend. For his family's sake. For our sakes, hear us."

"Hear us, Yahweh. Surely you can change my brother's heart."

Abishai grabs hold of you and starts hugging you, sobbing. You have no choice but to hang on as his grip crushes you. After a few minutes he begins to relax, resting his face on your chest. You hold him until he stops and pulls back, leaving wet blotches on the front of your robe.

"Sorry, sire, I . . ."

"Perfectly fine . . ."

"Don't tell the men . . ."

"I won't."

" . . . or I'll have to show them how old you're getting."

"Wouldn't dream of it. You're a man worthy of all the honor I could give you in front of your men."

"Thank you . . . my king. Umm . . . goodnight."

He walks out the door faster than you can think up something to say. Man, he's quick. You're thankful you've never had to fight *against* him. You sit amazed at what just happened. As your thoughts turn to Joab, a voice interrupts you . . .

"Sire?" Abishai's head pops back in the door.

"Yes?"

"Do you think . . . ? Do you think he'll . . . ?"

" . . . change? I hope so, but I don't know. You know you can't make that happen. All you can be responsible for is you."

"But I can ask Yahweh, right? . . . and sing the song?"

"Ask Yahweh as much as you can, every day. He loves it when you do, and not just about Joab. You can talk to Him about everything . . . about your father." You look at each other in understanding. "But, as for the singing . . . You'd better leave that to me."

"But I *like* the song."

"But you can't sing!" You bust out laughing, but Abishai keeps looking at you without flinching. You stop, awkwardness lasting for two seconds longer than's comfortable.

"You don't think I sing well? I've never done it . . . I guess maybe . . ."

You put your arm around him, "I was only joking, Bish. Sing it all you want! You serious about never singing before?"

He gives you *the* look. "Told you never to call me Bish."

"Oh . . . right . . . sorry, Abishai. I forgot. Hey, really," you grab him by the shoulders and look him in the eye, "really, thanks for coming. Keep praying and singing for your bro'. He needs as many honorable warriors like you on his side as possible."

Abishai's face lightens. His eyes start glowing with a look you've never seen. If you didn't know better, you'd think he was happy.

"Gotta get back to my bunk, get a few hours in before roll call. You better get some sleep, too, my king."

He bounds out for good. You put away the harp and climb into bed. You ask Yahweh again to get through to Joab, and thank Him for the joy you see in Abishai. And then you fall asleep.

Are you Abishai or Joab

If you've already read the story of Absalom, you know all about Ahithophel and his tragic end. If not, go back to the end of the last chapter and look up the reference I told you to. Seriously, the stories of David are cool adventures. Plus, the Bible's a pretty good book, with lots of great quotes.

Check out 1 Samuel 26 all the way to 1 Kings 2 for the full story of Joab and Abishai. Joab, though head of David's army, had the nasty habit of murdering anyone who he perceived to be a threat to David or his career (Abner, Absalom, and Amasa). When Solomon became king, Joab didn't die well.

Abishai was with David when he could have killed Saul in a cave (1 Samuel 24). He listened when David told him not to touch the Lord's anointed. He became chief over David's mighty men, the most lethal warrior in all of Israel. Although he pursued Abner with Joab for killing his brother, Asahel, it was Joab who deceived and killed Abner later on his own. Although Abishai wanted to kill Shimei for cursing David as he was fleeing Absalom, he again obeyed David and left him unharmed.

After Joab violated David's orders and killed Absalom, David began entrusting more of the army to Abishai. He saved an older David from a Philistine who was about to kill him, the last time David went out to battle. Abishai's death is never mentioned. He seems to have died honorably.

The love of God can change even the harshest of men in the most dysfunctional families. It will also let you die in misery if you choose to rely on your strength to increase your own glory. Do your actions look more like Abishai's or Joab's?

The Psalm 42–36 connection. A lucky guess or . . . ?

I wrote the chapter for Psalm 42 first, and had picked Psalm 36 to write next purely by chance. As I began reading Psalm 36, I immediately thought of Joab and Abishai and how their back-story and the chapter I'd just written fit so perfectly. I had no idea at the time that some scholars believe that David wrote Psalm 36 about Ahithophel after Absalom's rebellion. If that's true, there's no way he wasn't also thinking about Joab's continual descent to the dark side, and his ultimate doom.

Follow-up questions

1. What's your relationship like with *your* father?
2. What do you think causes some people to choose God's mercy while others consistently choose to rely on themselves?
3. How much do your choices and actions affect God's emotions?

Finding Your Sight

Way out of the realm in which my eyes perceive,
Stretching beyond the bounds of this locked down, set in place,
    physical reality,
More than I can run, drive, fly, reach, smell, feel, or dream,
Past the limits of my mental maze, analytical gaze, blazing fast and
    farther than the rays of starlight's firstborn gleam,
All surrounding, touching the beginning and dreaded ending of
    my spirit's eternity,
Close to me, is Your mercy.

Never giving up, not even close to breaking down,
Always the last one to bolt for the door, even when I'm not around.
You've been here or there, wherever my quick steppin', shifty slide
    decided outcome landed this ridiculous looking clown.
Tryin' to get away would be like trying to outjump a rocket ship
    with glue stuck to the bottom of my shoes.
I'd lose a height contest with Your inescapable presence faster than
    a dwarf with a magic beanstalk shooting up to the clouds.
You're so real it vaporizes the meteors of my doubt,
Throws them out with the trash of everything I could hope to
    imagine, conjure, or pretend,
My faithful Friend.

I'm defended in my weakness,
Overwhelmed by Your mountainous strength,
Towering peaks of mighty goodness challenge me to assault their
    steadfast, anchored flanks,
The lengths I could dig and never find an end to Your treasured
    mines filled with dazzling emerald caves, crested waves of pure,
    innocent, unchangingly kind thoughts.
My mouth drops in wonder,
Hits my knees like trees crashing to the ground,

How Do You "Bless" the Lord? – Psalm 103

How do you "bless" the Lord? It's easy to see how He blesses you, but you blessing Him? He's kinda got everything (pause for effect of understatement).

If you were to "bless" someone, you'd speak words of affirmation and encouragement over them. You'd verbally praise their good traits and accept them for who *they* are. Combine it with actions and service to them, and they would only love you more.

Turns out that God delights in encouragement, too. Your affirmation touches His heart. It brightens His eyes. Makes Him smile. Big, authentic, eye-twinkling smile.

It's not like God depends on your encouragement for His well-being. But He's opened Himself up to you. Not only is He touched by you, you're changed by blessing Him. You see truth more vividly than doubt. Joy becomes more real than despair.

Remind yourself of all that God constantly does for you. Don't take for granted all the good He does for you, personally. That's where Psalm 103 starts.

❋   ❋   ❋

You're standing in Jerusalem with those who've returned from captivity in Babylon. The new Temple's finally finished, and everyone's gathered to celebrate. Haggai stands at the front, encouraging everyone how God was the One who helped them finish. He's just finished introducing the singers and musicians who will begin worship at the Temple day and night, just like they did in King David's time. Now he turns it over to them. A hush falls on the crowd.

The temple worshipers begin with a choir of voices, speaking . . .

Soul, bless Yahweh, and everything inside me, bless His matchless name.
Soul, bless Yahweh, and don't forget all He deserves.

Those lines command you. They pinball around your heart while a slow, triumphant march begins. Your mind floods with images of everything God deserves: sacrifice, offerings, thanksgiving, tithes. Different soloists sing or speak each line along with the music . . .

The One who pardons your depravity, the One who heals all your diseases,
The One who becomes your close relative to buy you back from death,
The One who surrounds you with faithfulness and compassions,
The One who fills the delight of your heart with good things so your youth is renewed like an eagle.
Yahweh's the One who gives truth and justice to all who are oppressed.
He gave Moses the knowledge of His paths and the sons of Israel His deeds.
Yahweh is compassionate and gracious, slow to anger with much kindness.
He won't accuse us until the end of time, nor will He keep our guilt.
He didn't act like our sins, nor did He give us the sentence of our depravity.
For as high as the sky is above the earth, so great is His kindness to those who stand in awe of Him . . .

The singers stop. The music pauses, before returning to the beginning. You can't fit a being like that in your head. "I thought this was going to be about what we're supposed to give Him, but I *want* to do something good for a God like that. He's so patient with people who accept Him *and* people who reject Him. He'd make Himself my family and take on whatever punishment I deserve to buy me back from death." Before you start to process it all, the chorus begins again. You hear it reflecting the first chorus, but from God's point of view . . .

> Just as a father has compassion for his sons, Yahweh has compassion on those who stand in awe of Him.
> He intimately knows our clay structure. He remembers that we're dust.
> Human days blossom like grass, like a flower in a field.
> The wind carries it away, and it's gone. The place where it stood never sees it again.
> But the kindness of Yahweh goes from forever to forever on those who stand in awe of Him, and His justice to all future generations,
> To those who closely guard His covenant and remember to apply His principles.
> Yahweh has fixed His throne in the sky and His royal power rules everything.

Your legs buckle. The God who rules everything is tender to you like the world's best father is to his favorite son . . . but better. He knows every aspect of your frailty. He shares His kindness forever. Even destruction of the Temple and the captivity couldn't stop His covenant with Israel. His love will transform every one of your children, if . . . if . . .

You try to mentally say the next few words, but tears and emotions flood your heart. "The God of everything took the lowest place in making a covenant with us. He took upon Himself the consequences when He made a forever agreement with Abraham. He doesn't require me to be perfect, but to remember that *He's* the source of my perfection. He cares more about it than I do. And He can make it happen, because His power's bigger and stronger than anything in the universe!"

The singers have stopped. The music stalls into just a few twinkles while you process the enormity . . . and then they explode together in joyous finale . . .

Bless Yahweh, all His strong and mighty messengers, who listen for the sound of His word and perform it.
Bless Yahweh, all His armies, who serve Him and perform His will.
Bless Yahweh, all His creation, in every place where He rules.
Bless Yahweh, my soul!

You throw your hands to the sky, forgetting everyone around you. If your heart was a firework, you'd shoot it to explode in reds, blues, purples, and gold. Every time He's rescued you, each pleasure, each comfort pours out of your mouth and movements in thankfulness. Somehow you feel Him enjoying you, dancing with you, pouring out tears of connection. You don't want it to end. But the feelings subside. You calm down, peace bathing you like your favorite pair of sandals.

Once you've calmed down, you begin to think about the words. You marvel at the way verses 3–10 parallel verses 12–18, backwards and forwards. Verses 12 and 18 mirror each other and verses 3 and 10. Verses 13 and the second half of 17 mirror each other and verses 4 and 9, and so on. Verses 11 and 19 also connect, like ending statements, proving that God's power comes from His love. Even the writing genius shows that God's only done good to you and deserves your blessing.

It makes you want to tell your neighbors, tell your friends, "God deserves blessing from the whole world!"

"Oh yeah, the final line. He deserves blessing from me." You pause, remembering how good He's been. You marvel that you could affect His heart. "I *want* to give Him blessing from all of me" and you fall even deeper in love with the way He loves all men, women, children, Israel, everyone . . . and just you.

Follow-up questions

1. In what ways do you regularly bless the Lord?
2. In what ways does God regularly bless you?
3. Do you have to feel like blessing the Lord when you do it? Why or why not?

Bless the Lord

Bless the Lord.
Bless the Lord, oh, my soul.
Bless the Lord.
Bless the Lord, oh, my soul.

Soul, don't forget.
Don't let the daggers of regret,
The hammers of not yet
Destroy all His whispers of truth.

He untwists all our depravity.
The healing in His hands makes diseases flee.
On the brink of ruin, He rescues the weak
With kindness that shines in our hearts.

(Chorus 2x)
Bless the Lord.
Bless the Lord, oh, my soul.
Bless the Lord.
Bless the Lord, oh, my soul.

Compassion flows from His smiling face
Filling mouths with love's pure taste,
Refreshing the weary who've run the race,
Sweet elixirs that soar into heaven.

Gaze on Him who rights wrongs of all oppressed.
Freedom marches in songs from slaves confessed.
Through failure He sees His children's best,
Slow to anger, rich in mercy.

(Chorus 2x)
Bless the Lord.
Bless the Lord, oh, my soul.
Bless the Lord.
Bless the Lord, oh, my soul.

He disciplines less than we deserve,
Wrath and anger conquered with tender words.
Beyond heaven's grasp, imaginations burst
With wonder to be called Beloved.

Fly from east to west, you won't find your sin.
Little children, your heart has conquered Him.
In your weakness, He quiets raging winds,
For He knows what His hands have fashioned.

(Chorus 2x)
Bless the Lord.
Bless the Lord, oh, my soul.
Bless the Lord.
Bless the Lord, oh, my soul.

People fade in the light of the setting sun,
Like a memory lost in oblivion,
But God's mercy refreshes His righteous ones
Flowing favor and goodness forever.

Bless the Lord, mighty angels, who rejoice in His word.
Bless the Lord, every worshiper throughout the earth.
Bless the Lord, all that exists through space and time,
Unleash art. Pour out music, He deserves our lives!

Bless the Lord . . .   (don't let us forget)
Bless the Lord, oh my soul,
Bless the Lord . . .   (let loose your thankfulness!)
Bless the Lord, oh my soul,
Bless the Lord . . .   (receive our showers of love, oh God)
Bless the Lord, oh my soul,
Bless the Lord . . .   (You deserve all our affection, our desire, our
    lives)
Bless the Lord, oh my soul.

You Can't Help But Feeeeel It – Psalm 148

It's time to get down.
Let it speak to ya down in ya soul.
James Brown, put on yo Jesus slippers!
Get the band rockin',
Make my booty shake to a beat!
Somethin' make me move
Make ya sweat in the heat.
It's time to get ready. It's time to get right.
Everybody gonna praise the Lord in this place tonight.

Now let's stop right there. You thought I forgot the story, didn't ya? I knew what I was doin'. Look at the behind the scenes meanin' of the word "praise" in "Praise the Lord!" 'Cause if we sayin' we gonna "praise the Lord," we gotta know what we mean when we say it. Can I get a witness? I said, CAN I GET . . . A WITNESS? (you're required to insert your "Amen" or other appropriate Christianese term right now.)

Okay. Calming down. Back to normal red-head mode. Psalm 148 can't be spoken or sung quietly. It wouldn't have been back in the day either. Out of the seven Hebrew words for praise, the one you see here almost all the way through is *halal*. It's exuberant, loud, joyful, even clamorously foolish praising. Had the writers meant the silent, calm, meditative praising, they would have used a different word. You feel me?

This psalm starts with a command to unleash your exuberance and love to Yahweh, the God who makes everything exist. That's everybody everywhere. No one's excluded or gets to claim that it's just not their personality. Then it focuses on two groups: beings in the heavenly realm (vv.1–6), and beings on earth (vv.7–12).

Ancient people didn't think of the heavens as "up there" or in outer space. It was like another dimension. A cosmic being was responsible for the wind, the sun, and every other force in nature. The closest we could come to it in our current thinking is the spiritual realm. Many native, or aboriginal, peoples still think this way. If you really want to understand them, look up a culture with an "animistic" worldview and go live with them for a while.

Until you do, try to think of everything mentioned in verses 1–6 as beings with personality. It follows a list from most powerful down to least powerful. The heights include all the beings who only live in the cosmic realm, kind of like Mount Olympus or Zion. Then it goes to angels and hosts, God's agents and armies that work in heaven or in the created universe. The sun, moon, and stars have direct effect on the earth but were seen as created beings that gave light and regulated the seasons. Finally the writer gets to the heaven of heavens and the cosmic waters that existed above the skies. These worked like the final barrier between heaven and the physical realm.

So all of you heavenly beings, get crazy loud and wild in celebrating God, because He created you. Without Him you wouldn't exist. He gave you power and glory that endures throughout time. And He set the boundaries that limit what you're able to do. You owe Him your allegiance.

Verse 7 starts with earthly things we have little interaction with, understanding of, or control over and slowly zeroes in on people great and small. First it's sea monsters and fish. Then the weather, followed by mountains, hills, and all kinds of plants. Next, all the animals and birds get included in the command to celebrate the Lord.

Finally come people in authority, men and women, old and young. The entire earth gets covered by this command to get wild and funky with God. Here's why . . .

Verse 13 says that He's the only one whose name will blow your mind with how good it is. It's not trying to say that Yahweh sounds the coolest. They thought of names as encompassing the character and functions of God. So His power, love, humility, and faithfulness are better than anything else in the heavens or on earth. In fact, by not naming any other gods, the writer(s) say that they're nothing compared to Yahweh. Don't think about worshiping them, 'cause you'd be wasting your time.

And then the final verse shows God's compassion and close relationship to us like a daddy to his kids. You can imagine the great ruler of the universe stepping out of His cosmic glory to share it with His people. "Exalting the horn" is like saying "giving them a place of dignity and honor." He does this for everyone who joins in the giant celebration in His awe-inspiring presence (that's what *tehilah*, the word for praise that's used there, means), for the nation of Israel and for all who stay near to Him. That's what He's really after: us being close and united with His love. How close do you let Him get to you?

Now if that ain't worth a giant, gospel choir get down, I don't know what is.
Time to let go yo' inhibitions,
Hike up yo' jeans,
Show me what funky means,
Shake yo' hips,
Tinglin' in yo' fingertips,
Do it in yo' office,
Sing crazy while you home,
Groove to the pulsin' in yo' eardrums,
Pick up that Holy Spirit telephone.
Everybody praise the Lord,
His power and mercy can't get ignored,
Everybody praaaiise the Looooorrrr-d.

Follow-up questions

1. Are there really cosmic beings in charge of the wind or is that just ancient superstition? Why or why not?
2. How do plants, animals, and the rest of creation get wild and funky praising the Lord?
3. What would a "place of dignity and honor" look like for you? Do you think He'd do that for you, or is that just for ancient Israel?

Praise the Lord Get Down

Is anybody with me that's ready to use their voice?
It's time to let go all our problems and let our spirits rejoice!
I'm here to sing hallelujahs to the mighty and glorious One,
And ain't nobody leavin' till all the glorifyin' gets done.

C'mon, who you gonna worship?
(Praise the Lord)
Who you gonna praise?
(Praise the Lord)
Way up above the cloudy skies
(Praise the Lord)
In the highest place.
(Praise the Lord)

Praise Him all that bear good news
(Praise the Lord)
And angels too.
(Praise the Lord)
All you bright and glittering armies
(Praise the Lord)
Shine 'cause He made you.
(Praise the Lord)

Praise Him, sun and moon,
(Praise the Lord)
Praise Him stars at night.
(Praise the Lord)
He reaches to the edge of the universe
(Praise the Lord)
And fills it with His light.
(Praise the Lord)

Has anyone ever found a place where the name of the Lord should
    not be praised?
He set limits to the sea, wove the rhythm of the world, and He lives
    from age to age.
Has anyone ever found a land where His big, strong hand doesn't
    save the weak?
He puts the homeless in a home, comforts children all alone, and is
    found by the ones who seek Him.

Praise Him all you rocks!
(Praise the Lord)
And the monsters in the deep.
(Praise the Lord)
Fire and hail, snow and vapor, stormy wind He keeps.
(Praise the Lord)

To the mountains and their peaks!
(Praise the Lord)
To the valleys with their fruit,
(Praise the Lord)
All the beasts and cattle
(Praise the Lord)
Birds and crickets play their flutes.
(Praise the Lord)

You kings better rule justly.
(Praise the Lord)
You judges judge in truth.
(Praise the Lord)
You young men and women,
(Praise the Lord)
Elderly and the youths,
(Praise the Lord)

Praise the name of Jehovah,
(Praise the Lord)
For He's the only One,
(Praise the Lord)
His greatness more than we can fathom.
(Praise the Lord)
He's called us daughters and sons.
(Praise the Lord)

Has anyone ever found a place where the name of the Lord should
   not be praised?
He sets His people high above, we're the children that He loves,
   and He lives from age to age.
Has anyone ever found a land where His loving hands couldn't
   make us free?
He's calling nations to His throne, we will never be alone, start the
   everlasting jamboree!

Oh, every culture, every people sing out the music of your heart.
Everybody feel His joy tearin' darkness apart.
Was there ever any doubting in that tiny seed of faith?
Just give it up to Him, 'cause He'll cleanse your past of sin, and He
   turns it into praise.

Praise the name of the Lord. (*slow and drawn out*)
(Praise the Lord) (*slow response*)

It's Good to Be Tiny – Psalm 8

Long ago my pastor told a story in the church where I grew up about an ant mound he played near as a child. Construction threatened them, and he wanted to save his tiny ant friends. So he imagined making himself into an ant, learning to speak ant language, and leading them to safety. The point of his story was the compassion and risk that a Savior took to rescue us. But I wonder how powerless the ants felt when they realized the enormity of the bulldozers and dump trucks about to squash them.

Whenever I begin contemplating the size and grandeur of the universe, I feel tinier and more powerless than those ants. At least they have mandibles and poison that can penetrate human skin. I can't do anything to stop a black hole, much less the God who created them and the rest of the universe. That never makes me jump up and down in happy happy joy. I'm humbled. It makes me stop in silence.

But joy is exactly the mood of Psalm 8. It says it's "upon gittith" or "on the instrument of Gath." Three psalms contain this inscription: Psalm 8, 81, and 84. It's not actually referencing a Philistine city. It literally means winepress. The words connect with a song they used whenever they gathered grapes to make wine. That's no time to contemplate the futility of life. That's when you kick your shoes off and celebrate 'cause you just can't help but feel good.

The music starts, flutes piping merrily. Drums start your feet kickin'. It's fast. You can't help but dancing . . .

Oh, Yahweh, our Lord,
All earth displays Your perfection,
The heavens rejoice with Your fame!
Your strength resides in an infant's smile
To conquer the rage of an enemies' bile.

You laugh at the thought of chubby little lips stopping the fury of madmen with swords, but there's no time to think. The music keeps racing . . .

When I look at the vastness of space,
The actions your fingers have traced,
The moon, the stars, Jupiter, Mars,
They fly at the pace that You've set.
Why would You let Your brain waste time on men?
Why would You stoop low to greet us like friends?
We're lower than angels,
But You crown us as kings
You made us to rule
And take power over all things,
All livestock and sheep,
What's wild and what creeps . . .

Your brain and muscles urge you to stop and consider the humbling power of these statements, but the drums won't let you. The trumpets and strings keep hoppin' . . .

Birds soar in the sky
Fish swim in the sea
Great ocean ships sail
And the duty to represent You resides within me.
Oh, Yahweh, our Lord,
All earth displays Your perfection,
The heavens rejoice with Your fame!

You shout and leap as the music soars on. It's so good they play it eleven more times, once for every tribe. When it ends, you fall down exhausted, excited about God . . . and doing nothing but resting until the pain in your body subsides.

It's not until a couple days later that it hits you. "The duty to represent You resides within me." You celebrated so hard you couldn't think, but now your eyes light up again.

"All the other gods I've heard of use their power to control me, make me serve them, and do what they want. Yahweh shares His power with me freely. He's too good to be true! No amount of rejoicing's enough to celebrate our King!" You feel silly with no music, dancing like a loon. But the happy happy joy has infected your body. You can't keep it under control. It's hard to fit inside your head. "But if we sang it, it must be . . ."

It's true. You're way more important than an ant to God. Of all the things He's created, He's reserved a special place in His heart that only you can touch. Don't spend too much time thinking about how tiny you are. Think about how wonderful and close He is.

Because I wrote the poem first . . .

I wrote the following performance piece before I looked at Psalm 8 more closely and wrote this story. If it seems darker and more desperate than the happy dancing tone I've described, that's because I approached it with more view of my frailty compared to God's grandeur. I hope you're okay with that. If not, you'll just have to write your own song, play, poem, story, or movie, maybe create a dance, sculpture, culinary or painting masterpiece as a more accurate interpretation (tongue sticking out at you . . . in a spirit of love, sorta).

Follow-up questions

1. What makes you feel small and powerless?
2. Who or what do you think God wants you to be or do?
3. What would you make your top priority if God made you the ruler of an entire kingdom?

When I Consider

When I consider the heavens,
The work of Your hands,
What is man,
That You would care?
That You would tear open the fabric of the universe,
Scrape yourself through
Just to be near,
Look me in the eye,
Pry me out of the bear trap of slavery before I die.

I don't see what You do when I stare at my reflection.
Introspection only exposes flaws,
Disgust creeping up my neck,
Pulling me down,
Drowning out sight,
The drone of never being good enough,
Fists pounding wounds,
Hair ripped out,
Razor sharp cuts,
Red ruts could never spill enough to quench this thirst,
Addiction's curse the only music my experience understands.
Are You strong enough to still my destructive plans?

Plant Your seed of what it means to be a man,
The work of Your hands,
More costly than the heavens,
Dearer than the death of one You love,
Nearer than a kiss to fire my blood.
Flood these veins with shooting stars.
Surge through cracks and scars.
Fashion instruments the world has never seen

From broken things,
Cast-off notes,
Rejected hopes and dreams,
New melodies singing peace,
Tone-deaf choirs drowning out fear,
Featherbeds made of recycled arrows and spears.
I don't need a magic halo or pristine wings.
Just let me sit at Your feast
Where homeless men and girls with eating disorders sit as kings
    and queens.

My lone voice
Swims with six billion seas of hope,
Past noisy waves on shores and radios,
Across the silent vacuum of space,
Beyond supernovas and unimagined colors
All the way to the threshold of Your ears . . .
But You already came near.
Your arms race to hold,
Voice soothes,
Hand stifles the breath of condemning lies,
Even what justice knows I deserve.
Archangels stare in awe.
Evil collapses in disbelief.

What have I done to receive such attention?
Your close and near connection.
Incomprehensible perfection.
My chest comes undone trying to fathom Your affection
For every work of art You've made . . .
And me,
This pile of rags declared beautiful,
Loveable skin,

Acceptable face,
Tender embrace.
Honor is the only fabric You know how to make for my
    clothes.

When I consider the heavens,
The work of Your hands
What is man?
Only You know.
You always love first.

Including the Parts the Pastor Doesn't Like – Psalm 90

Moses wrote this psalm, and on the first few reads I didn't get it. There's God being the ultimate place to go for help and being the ultimate God. Yay! It's easy to write and sing songs in church about stuff like that. Then comes destruction, frailty, evil, sin, and wrath. You don't usually hear that on Sunday morning. How does that fit with the nice part?

Then comes the poetic stuff at the end that writers really love. "Satisfy us early with Your mercy, that we may rejoice and be glad all our days" (NKJV). So beautiful! But it ends with a less than impressive statement that twice says to "establish the work of our hands" (NKJV). Maybe Moses had a different style than the other Hebrew poets that was more like Mesopotamian or even Egyptian writers?

Nope. Read it again. There's a beginning (vv.1–6), middle (vv.7–12), and end (vv.13–17). The progression of each one of these sections parallels each other, if you look closely. When I followed these parallel thoughts they struck me with their literary beauty and even more with what they tell me about God and my relation to Him.

So start with the first section. Here Moses talks about God and how He compares to us. He's the place to turn to, the constant that you can rely on forever. Before creation, He exists. After this world ends, He exists. Nothing that goes on escapes His knowledge. He's way more solid than the Matterhorn's towering face or the granite of

El Capitan in Yosemite National Park. He's stronger than the light of every star.

When he says, "You turn man to destruction" (NKJV), Moses isn't saying that God destroys man. He's saying, "You show man his coming destruction and say, 'Don't go that way! Come back to Me! I want to rescue you and be close, not destroy you.'" The judgment of God is very real, but it's His last resort.

Moses follows this up by talking about the way God can change the course of history in one day, for good or ill. Has it been sunny, bright, and prosperous for a thousand years? He can snuff it out instantly. Have you suffered for what seems like endless agony? He can put joy in your heart so powerful that you forget the pain of your past. The poetic images of the past being like sleep, carried away like a flood, as temporary as the grass, drive home the reality of our temporary situation in light of God's everlasting existence. Do you want God or yourself to be in control of your life?

The second section displays the human perspective. Compare it to the parallel thoughts of verses 1–6. Moses starts throwing bombs into our self-confidence. Verse 7 collides with verse 1. Verse 8 collides with verse 2, and so on. They line up so perfectly the only way you'd miss his point is to be reading a translated copy in a completely different culture.

He's trying to tell you that it's foolishness trying to live life without God. When you go your own way His anger seems everywhere. Instead of having Him as your refuge, God's power dismays you. "Why does He seem to be against me?" It's because the secret intentions of your heart can't hide from Him. Lust gets exposed. Hatred sticks out its ugly tongue. Selfishness destroys the people you were made to love.

God sees it all. Your life crashes into His everlasting goodness and falls flat. You end with a whimper. If you make it to seventy or eighty years, that seems like a full life, but in the light of history, you don't seem to make much difference. All your efforts will one day blow away with the slightest breeze. Who knows how powerful God truly is? He could end the universe with a thought. Do you really want to fight against that?

"So teach us to number our days," Moses says (NKJV). You can look at all of man's problems and lack of impact and get depressed, or you can consider what really matters each day. Everything you do is important, especially looking at our short lives that end so unexpectedly. If you turn your eyes back to God's everlasting refuge, to His call to be near Him, you'll be wiser. If you keep your eyes on yourself, you'll live life struggling, frustrated, and restless.

Moses' concluding section begins boldly in verse 13: "Return, O Lord!" (NKJV) He's revealed that we're the ones that need to turn back to God. But the way you do that is by acknowledging that you can't make it on your own. You need God to move His refuge, His home to you. "We can't wait another thousand years. We want you today!" he says with the question of "How long?" "And have compassion on your servants" (NKJV).

He continues this longing for God in verse 14: "Satisfy us early with your mercy" (NKJV). Now that part's poetic in English. In Hebrew it must have been even more stunning, especially in comparison with verse 2's, "Before the mountains were brought forth . . ." (NKJV). It's almost as if Moses is saying, "God, could You go back before we were born and undo all our mistakes? Could you rewrite our history? Take away the evil intent and secret sin of verse 8 and replace it with rejoicing and gladness for our entire life."

"Turn all the past into joy. For every year of evil, give us gladness that swallows it up. Instead of our lives passing away in futility, show us Your deeds, God. Let the full blaze of Your beauty capture the hearts of generations down the line. This isn't just for us, it's for children to come." Sounds like a good way to take your eyes off yourself and develop good intentions for others.

Moses doesn't just want the black and white of law. He wants God's beauty. He's referencing God's plan for the Garden of Eden to grow, multiply, and cover the earth. If you get God's heart implanted in you, His beauty will radiate from your every action.

He'll transform society. He'll make your labor fruitful, lasting, worthwhile.

You want to live for a cause that's worth it? Ask the God who lasts forever to come put His heart in yours. He'll make your life an inspiration to others, no matter how menial your work. He'll empower you to stare down rejection, despair, and the pain of life and come out on the other side with more joy for you and everyone around you.

Dang. Another incredible psalm. I haven't found a dud yet. It's like they were all chosen precisely because they're so amazing. Hopefully you'll have the courage to write, and live, more than just the easy parts to understand.

Follow-up questions

1. What's the most powerful thing (good or bad) you've ever done in your life?
2. If God could rewrite any part of your history, what would you have Him change?
3. How much does it affect others when you start living with all of God's beauty radiating from you?

Coming Home

God, You've been our home
Before oceans to the land gave birth.
Before the fabric of the universe, You called the earth.
When ages end, the stars expire,
You still remain. Unending choirs proclaim
You're greater, stronger, wonder of everything.
Forever Your voice resounds
A beacon of rest.
Stress just melts away,
Emptiness satisfied,
Addiction's voice dead in the ecstasy of true desire.
We could ignite our fires, burn it all,
Or receive Your unassuming call,
"Return."
Tears wiped clean by joy.
Bitter memories lost in childhood wonder.
Ten thousand years of achievement melt like dew in the heat of
  sun.

God, we've been alone,
Terrified of Your anger, far from home.
Our dark intentions nail their curse
Far below the skin, too deep to scratch.
Monsters crawl out with each new batch of rules we brew.
To do lists. Impotent vows.
Our burdens bow us,
Staggering along a restless path.
We've traded Your love for fear of Your wrath.
Our years drone lifeless, hollow-eyed stares,
A tunnel that never shines hope,
Robbed of our future,
Numb to the past,

Efforts expiring in death.
Please don't ever unlock Your rage.
Pull us close to Your ways.
Only Your perspective brightens our days.

God, make us Your home.
Hear our desperate groans. Woo our hearts of stone.
Remove the thorn of shame and pride
That separates us from tender hands,
Compassionate glances healing the past,
Rewriting a future with music, laughter,
Choirs that split open rafters above,
Chains off our souls,
Memories that whisper no pain.
Let Your might carve a brand new kingdom of rest,
Children celebrating the warmth of Your face.
Don't just turn wrong to right.
Unleash your splendor.
Invent colors.
Cascade beauty.
Let every eye drink the music of dancing stars.
Then peace will marry our hearts,
An eternity of desire fulfilled.

Fragrant Oil Bath for You, Friend? – Psalm 133

You've probably never covered your beard in oil (or maybe you've never had a beard!). Never dreamed of happiness in terms of fragrant gooeyness running down your face and clothes. You probably have no idea what it's like on Mount Hermon or how good the dew must feel when it descends. The only useful parts of Psalm 133 seem like the first verse and the very end. What the heck are you supposed to do with the middle?

Why don't we just shorten it? Then we'd have "How good and pleasant it is when brothers dwell together in unity. There the Lord commands the blessing, life forevermore." Great psalm. Makes sense. But God isn't just rational. He's an artist, a lover, a party host who specializes in overloading your senses with decadence . . .

Something miraculous happens when believers live together in harmony. No writer would settle for describing that with simple words like "good" and "pleasant". But this is a song of ascents, building and growing with each line. It plants a seed of understated niceness, and blossoms with mystery, holiness, and extravagance.

In ancient times men used to anoint their head and beard with fragrant oils. It was better than deodorant. Not only did it smell good, it indicated wealth and prosperity. The more fragrant oil, the more status and honor you conveyed to everyone who came close enough to catch your scent.

And if that wasn't enough, the priests applied a sacred anointing oil before they went into the tabernacle or temple. They weren't allowed into the presence of God without it. The Law also stated that no one else could make any anointing oil like it. It was the costliest of oils. The only time anyone ever smelled it meant that you had come close to the presence of the Creator of the universe. Even a tiny drop meant you had been set apart for the service of God.

But Psalm 133 doesn't say that God portions out tiny packets of His presence. He starts with it on the head, pours it until it spills over onto your clothes. He deluges you with the blessing of community before unlocking the door to look Him in the eye. Your skin tingles. He reveals the secrets of His heart. You become someone worthy of honor and respect.

As if that wasn't enough, the writer whisks you off to the mountains east of Jerusalem. Everyone in Israel would have instantly known about Mount Hermon. Israel's highest peak, it glows with scenic beauty. Fog covers it in the wintertime and develops overnight in summer. It hangs in the air, more dense than the mist of the Great Smoky Mountains of the United States, or the Blue Mountains of Australia. Anyone visiting gets surrounded by water vapor. The snow that falls there in winter skips down the mountain to water the surrounding countryside.

That's what God's blessings are like in the context of relationship. His goodness hunts you down. His kindness refreshes your heart. His love satisfies thirsty souls. To make sure that no one mistakes this as a temporary condition, the writer throws out the image of the mountains of Zion, the place where God lives. Imagine Mount Olympus, but with a God who's far above the petty arguments and scandals of Greek mythological figures.

The Cornerstone of life proclaims too much joy, thrills that leave you aching for more adventure, deeper passion, a journey that lasts forever. The issuing of God's blessing begins your adventure with Him. And your ticket gets stamped when you put down your rights and disarm your tongue. God anoints your head with peace, drenches your life and everyone around you with fulfillment. He crowns you with favor that can never be revoked.

It sounds too good to be true. But whispers you can't deny tug on your spirit, urging you to give up your selfishness and pride. I can almost hear the earth groaning, like in Romans 8, for the revealing of the sons and daughters of God. Isn't that worth a little oil messing up your fancy clothes?

Follow-up questions

1. What would people think if you showed up at work, school, or wherever with oil covering your hair or clothes?
2. Which human alive is your best friend?
3. What would you have to change in the way you treat others to live in the kind of unity that Psalm 133 talks about?

More than Sharing

Exhale your stress.
Let out a sigh,
Hope surrounding each step you take,
Peace that an easy smile makes,
Brothers and sisters brightening at the sight of your face,
Chilly winds silenced by a warm embrace,
Flooded by laughter, harbored, safe,
Swimming in treasure that wealth can't create
When hearts find community waiting.

Angels descend.
Heaven creeps near,
Singing in ears,
Glowing from cheeks,
Flowing springs on mountain peaks
Cleansing old wounds,
Swallowing pride,
Dancing in toes,
Leaping to unseen heights,
Freedom discovered in laying down rights.

Father and mother,
Daughters and sons,
Strangers turned family.
Innocence crowns old and young,
Joy whispers to bones.
Loads leap off backs.
Loneliness powerless in all its attacks,
A garden of forgiveness,
Love refreshing parched throats.
God opens eternal treasure doors
When His children risk living as one.

You Have No Idea – Psalm 146

You have no idea how beautiful God is.

Neither do I.

Every time my eyes open to some new aspect of His character, I want to explode. I can't contain it. He's got to make my spirit stronger so my brain can handle the colors and sensations, more vivid, more ecstatic, sweet bliss. I can't help but fall in love with Him. I can't help but be awed that He would love me. If you've tasted the tiniest bit of His goodness, you know what I mean.

Have you ever read the part in Revelation where John gets overcome with the beauty of heaven, and falls down to worship the angel in front of him? If you haven't, check it out in Revelation 19 and 22. He does it twice! I've always wondered how a guy who spent so much time with Jesus and heard His heartbeat could get fooled. When I was looking at Psalm 146, I got some idea . . .

I was searching for the pattern the writer used, and, not really figuring it out (man, it'd be so much easier if you could hear the psalms with the music they originally composed!). I tried a couple different variations: two stanzas of five verses, stanzas of two, two, five and one verse. Maybe four, four, fourteen, and a triplet, if you make each little phrase inside a verse one line. (I know you're probably bored, but hang with me.) Nothing quite fit.

Then I noticed how the first two verses each have two phrases that compare to each other; a set of couplets. It's a declaration that he's going to give God the utmost praise from his heart for his whole life. The same happens with verses 3 and 4 and then verses 5 and 6. The only difference is the topics. Verses 3 and 4 warn us that expecting rulers or humans to save the world is like hoping for a dog to clean up your garden and live forever. Verses 5 and 6 point to the happiness of those who trust God, since He made everything and keeps it running smoothly forever. Hmmm . . . three couplets.

In verse 7 a change occurs. Each verse becomes a triplet, illustrating three aspects of God's character. They continue through verse 9, covering nine aspects of God's character in all. Verse 7 shows His justice, provision, and freedom. Verse 8 displays His revelation, honor, and love. Verse 9 lets us taste His protection, tenderness, and judgment. It's stunning to look at. That alone makes me want God forever. And then I thought, "Hmmm . . . another set of three, this time triplets."

The three couplets tell us that God is the One who structures the world and keeps it running. The three triplets tell us that He fills and regulates it and everything He created with all the virtues of His character. Every aspect flows out of His love. The only thing left is a final day, where God rests, enthroned in His home, receiving the honor He deserves forever. Sound like some other story in the Bible you've heard?

Oh, and look at that! A final triplet in verse 10 where God becomes King over all, takes His rest in the home (Zion) that He chose, and we worship, dance, celebrate, and explode our hearts to Him forever for all His goodness! (If you've ever seen *The Muppets*, you'll know why I feel just a bit like Kermit introducing a guest right now.)

Read over the psalm again in the arrangement I've described and paraphrased below. Try proving that it's not how the original writer intended it.

Shine clamorous praise to Yahweh!
Soul, shine clamorous praise to Yahweh!

I will shine clamorous praise to Yahweh while I remain alive.
I will make musical praise to my God continually.

Don't wrap your trust around rulers,
In the son of a man who gives no deliverance.
His breath expires, he returns to the ground,
In that moment his thoughts are extinguished.

How happy is he who has the God of Jacob as his rescue,
Whose hope is in Yahweh, his God.
Who fashioned the sky, the earth, the sea, and everything in them,
Who watches over them constantly forever.

Who fashions justice for the exploited
Who gives food to the hungry
Yahweh sets free those who are bound.

Yahweh gives revelation to the blind.
Yahweh straightens those who are bent down.
Yahweh loves the just.

Yahweh watches over foreigners.
He surrounds orphans and widows.
But He subverts the path of criminals.

Yahweh has become King forever.
This is your God, Zion, for generations and generations.
Shine your clamorous praise to Yahweh!

I should have known when I saw the reference to all of creation in verse 6.
The writer's given us a song telling us that we should praise God and put
our trust in Him over anyone else, *and* used the backdrop of the creation
story for it. The way the rhythm builds in the lines itself sweeps you away
into ecstatic delights of God. It declares that the world will come into

order when humans stop looking for heroes in and among ourselves and start looking at the King of everything. We'll have rest, satisfaction, and joy forever with Him. Add music, and I don't think I could take it. I'm blown away at the genius of whoever did this. I want to bow down before Him and . . .

See what I mean? Sometimes you see the beauty in someone and forget that it came from the One who made them in the first place. For millennia, men have marveled at the earth, the sky, and the glory of each creature, and worshiped some aspect of the universe, forgetting the One whose Word breathed it to life. Now we look at our technology, our scientific discoveries, our building of cities and monuments and imagine that we've evolved on our own to the top of the food chain. "I am the master of my fate: I am the captain of my soul." William Ernest Henley's *Invictus* says.

And all of creation, even our own minds and bodies, are screaming alongside the angel in Revelation, "Don't do that! I'm your fellow servant. Worship God . . ."

Look at Him. Look at how He loves. Nothing comes close to that. Don't be afraid to give yourself to Him. He'll never disappoint you.

You have no idea how beautiful He is.

Neither do I.

Follow-up questions

1. If you could be any historic figure or superhero, who would you choose? Why?
2. Which aspects (if any) about God are better than your chosen hero?
3. How often have you been disappointed by people? Yourself? God?

Don't Trust Barack Obama

Do not put your trust in Barack Obama.

No matter your inclination,

We've finally got an African American in the White House consecration,

Or scent of perspiration,

Don't you do it.

'Cause sure he's got those big-eared, good looks that no woman can deny,

He's a Harvard-educated guy,

And I hear he fries up anyone who opposes his health-care plan for breakfast,

But we all know he can't help me with the contents of my grocery list,

And those clever speechmaking tricks aren't the kind of fix my heart needs

When I'm feelin' lonely under a cloudy sky.

And let's face it, someday the boy won't be alive.

He's gonna die

Just like you and I and every parliament member who's chosen promoting their career over defending an innocent person's plight,

So don't get your hopes up, all right?

And while I'm at it,

Don't bet all your money on a bunch of horses,

No matter what kind of tip you squeezed from your inside sources,

'Cause that orange juice ain't fresh pressed,

Turns kinda bitter when Smarty Jones is stumblin' down the stretch,

And lord knows there hasn't been a triple-crown winner since the 70s,

And not even the rippling flanks of the majestic Secretariat,

Or the feel good story of Seabiscuit overcoming the odds seemed
    like a sure thing at the time,
So save yourself the peace of mind and put your money where
    your blind eyes can see it.

You know, come to think of it, you can't count on the weather,
The attraction of your chick magnet, pimpified, pleather pants,
An endless romance,
My math skills,
An endless stream of dollar bills,
Purple pills,
Or getting included in your grandfather's will.
You know you can't trust a Sicilian when death is on the line.
In fact, it seems death is the only thing really certain,
But that's completely depressing
And, it turns out, not even remotely true since it's already been
    conquered,
So what can you trust?

What if I could stop the rain,
Harness the clouds,
If the breath from my mouth sent innocent children playful
    dreams,
Wrapping them tenderly in the warmth of snuggly sheets?
What if my fingers dripped the dew,
Knew every flight of the soaring eagle,
Gave them food,
Could change the mood of the hopeless,
The defender of the fatherless,
Opening blind eyes,
Including the ostracized,
Healing the paralyzed?
What if I could make the dead come to life?!
And what if I left all that power in the skies

Just so I could be your friend,
No matter what it cost me in the end?
What if I limited myself to the frail form of my own creation
Risking rejection,
Hurled insults,
Pointed spears of suffering,
Inhuman torture,
Being left alone by everyone
Just so I could see your beautiful face again?

Would you trust Me then?

Not political at all

I originally wrote this piece during the presidency of George W. Bush and titled it, "Don't Trust George W." Below is how the original stanza went. Oh, and before I get ex-communicated for using the word "pants," please remember that in America, we call trousers pants. I tried to change it for the sake of any who can't stomach the image, but I would have had to rewrite about half the poem. (Besides, I had already changed a number of other perfectly dangerous lines in the book editing process to make it more acceptable.) Man, if two groups of people separated only 240 years ago who "speak the same language" experience that kind of misunderstanding, how amazing is it that God still speaks through the translation of poetry written 3,500 years ago in Israel!

Now to the first stanza in my original poem . . .

Do not put your trust in George W. Bush.
No matter your inclination,
Conservative consecration
Or scent of perspiration,
Don't you do it.

'Cause sure he's got those bumpkin good looks that no woman can
  deny,
He's a really smart guy,
And I hear he fries up third world nations who oppose him for
  breakfast,
But we all know he can't help me with, much less spell, the con-
  tents of my grocery list,
And those clever tax-cut tricks aren't the kind of fix my heart needs
When I'm feelin' lonely under a cloudy sky.
And let's face it, someday the boy won't be alive.
He's gonna die,
Just like you and I and his father's "thousand points of light,"
So don't get your hopes up, all right?

If Barack is not (or no longer) your leader, feel free to rewrite the
  first stanza.

Something Scary from My Real Life – Psalm 27

The following is an imagined conversation I had with my atheist friend, Keith, late at night while trying to finish this manuscript. If you've gotten this far, I think you'll like it. Just to be clear who's who, I speak first, and Keith speaks second. The rest you can figure out on your own . . .

"Remember the first full-on battle scene in *Braveheart*?"

"The part where William Wallace and a bunch of Scotsmen expose themselves to the English army?"

"No, after that, where they take on the English heavy cavalry."

"Oh, with the charge of the horses. Sure."

"Right. No infantry had ever been able to withstand a charge of heavy cavalry. But there stands William Wallace, surrounded by Scotsmen, ready to fight. The horses begin to charge. The distance between them begins to disappear. And instead of yelling 'fight!' or 'charge!' or 'run!' William Wallace says . . ."

"*Hold!*"

"Isn't it awesome?"

"It's ridiculous. He says it way too many times."

"Right up until the last moment . . ."

"*Hold!*" "It takes forever. Have you seen the parodies on YouTube?"

"Someone parodied it?"

"Look it up. There's a few of 'em. They get destroyed by the Death Star, a nuclear bomb, a Stargate SG-1 alien ship."

"But that's such a good scene. It ruins this whole illustration."

"Sorry. You know it's just a movie."

"A really inspiring movie."

"But come on, it's fake. They made up the whole story. They've got terrible accents. And you can tell they used dummy horses when he and the horse jump off the tower. The horse doesn't move at all while it falls. Look."

"Never mind the cool parallels I drew to Psalm 27 from it. Thanks a bunch, Keith."

"Well at least ya found out it sucks now. Just tell 'em something scary from your real life."

"My real life?"

"Yeah. Come on, what's the scariest thing that's ever happened to you? It's got to be pretty bad. People can relate to that stuff."

"But I've already talked about demons and witches in my dreams."

"Okay, the second scariest thing."

"Hmm . . . maybe it's one of three things."

"Like . . ."

"Like:

1. Having to admit a $250,000 mistake at Motorola in front of about 45 guys, all hungry to punish someone for screwing up their hard work.
2. Enduring the eleven-year-old humiliation of my entire sixth grade class laughing at me at school after I'd called out a super low math homework score.
3. Wondering where money was going to come from when I was $13,000 in debt and had no shows or work lined up for the rest of the year."

"Hmmm . . . those aren't that bad."

"Exactly."

"Real tough life you got."

"I know. Not anywhere close to the stuff you've faced."

"Eh, my life's pretty good."

"I know you've stared down the cruelty of bullies . . ."

"That ain't so bad. Some people get raped, abused. Ya got bombs, bullets, and genocide. What's Psalm 27 got to tell them?"

"You probably won't like it."

"Try me."

"You really want to know?"

"Tell me already!"

"Okay, okay. In the face of every one of those enemies, Psalm 27 says, 'Wait on the Lord . . .'"

"Are ya serious, Peter?"

"Yep."

"That's nuts! Whaddaya s'posed to do, get on your knees and let 'em walk all over ya?"

"No."

"Sure sounds like it."

"It's not saying to keep getting abused, or let someone just kill you. Rahab hid the spies. David fled from Saul. Elijah hid from Ahab and Jezebel. If you're being abused, get out. Do everything you can to protect yourself or those who are being abused. But don't take matters into your own hands and attack. Don't pretend that you can endure mistreatment. Find the people that God has prepared to shelter you and expect Him to take care of the oppressor in His time and by His means."

"So that's it."

"No. Just answering your question."

"Fine. Can you start with the psalm already?"

"Okay . . ."

Yahweh is my light and my salvation. Who should make me stand in awe?

Yahweh is the strong tower of my life. Who should I dread?

"Seriously, if the biggest, baddest Power in the universe that created everything, keeps it alive and working and made a nation out of a bunch of ungrateful slaves so that He could make a forever agreement with them that He would keep, why can't you trust Him?"

"Yeah, yeah, I get it."

"Found anyone better?"

"Keep going."

"Have you?"

"No. Now will ya keep reading?"

When those who do evil approached me to devour my flesh,
My adversaries and enemies staggered and fell.
Even if an army camp lays siege on me, my heart won't fear.
If war breaks out on me, in this I trust:

"And that happens by invisible magic?"

"You gonna keep interrupting me?"

"Fine. Read on."

One thing I've requested of Yahweh, and that's my desire:
To stay in the house of Yahweh my whole life,
To see Yahweh's beauty and seek His palace.

"Wait, really? You've got an army cutting off your food supply, waiting to cannibalize you, and you're gonna stay in an invisible house and look for God's beauty? Doesn't He have a whole army of angels with magic arrows and swords and stuff? Did ya skip a verse?"

"No. You missed the writer's perspective."

"It's *the Bible*. It's s'posed to just be true."

"Are you superstitious or something?"

"No, that's *your* religion."

"Nice. But you saying it's just supposed to be true is like me saying that Spider-Man isn't true because he got bit by a radioactive spider, and in the real world, people just die or lose an arm or somethin' when that happens."

"Spider-Man's a comic. This is *the Bible*."

"Maybe, but it sure inspires a bunch of people. And it assumes that there's evil in the world and someone's got to stand up against it and stop it."

"Okay, sure, but still, this is *the Bible*."

"C'mon, these were real people writing in a completely different culture and time. The spiritual world wasn't optional. It was the real world. If you wanted success, you better have the favor of the gods. Otherwise you're goin' down. That's why they scanned the sky and animal intestines for omens. They thought that the gods were sending messages. The best hope was to placate as many of them as possible."

"So how does that tie in with Psalm 27, to the holy people who don't believe in that stuff."

"It says you don't have to perform a ritual to placate God. You don't have to fix it on your own. If you've been terrorized, snuggle in His presence and stay there. If you're with Him, who would dare touch you? It was just as radical to them as it is to you."

"Okay, fine. Can you get back to the reading now?"

"Sure . . ."

For He will protect me like treasure in His hiding place in the time of calamity.
He will hide me in the shelter of His tabernacle.

He will raise me up on top of an unreachable cliff.
Now my head will rise above my enemies surrounding me.

And I will slaughter sacrifices in His tabernacle with a shout of triumph.
I will sing, yes, I will make musical praise to Yahweh.

"It was pretty good up to the slaughter sacrifices part. That's messed up."

"It's the same thing as giving money to a church or a non-profit organization. Animals were currency. Plus, to them sacrifices weren't just to cover sin, they were to gain favor, or to honor whichever deity they worshiped. In this case, Yahweh."

"And the shout of triumph? Is he victorious by killing a helpless animal?"

"No, he's saying that his shouts of praise are victorious battle cries. See, it's paralleled with singing and musical worship."

"Okay. I got it. C'mon . . . more."

"This is the second part, so you've got to line it up with the first part and compare 'em."

"Okay, great. *Keep going.*"

Hear when I call with my voice, Yahweh,
And show favor and respond to me.

You said to my heart, "Seek My presence,"
And I'm seeking Your presence, Yahweh.

"How does that line up with 'Yahweh is my light and my salvation . . .' and all?"

"Just read one right after the other."

"Like, 'Hear when I call with my voice, Yahweh . . . Yahweh is my light and my salvation. Who should make me stand in awe' . . . ?"

"Yep."

"And then 'And show favor and respond to me. Yahweh is the strong tower of my life. Who should I dread?'"

"See, sometimes it says the same thing when you do it. Sometimes it answers a question. But they always connect. They planned it that way."

"Maybe they were decent writers."

"They only did it all day, every day for their whole lives. The only way they wouldn't be good is if they were stupid . . . or less than human."

"Well they *did* believe the earth was flat."

"You consciously eat junk food."

"It tastes good."

"It slowly kills you."

"Whatever. Keep reading."

Don't hide Your presence from me.
Don't stretch Your servant out in anger.
You've become my help.
Don't leave me or abandon me, God who saves me.

"Sounds pretty needy."
"And you're not? I thought you wanted me to keep going?"
"Yeah, yeah. C'mon."

If my father and mother abandon me,
Yahweh will take me in.

Point out Your road, Yahweh,
And guide me in a level path, because of my *Sorek*.

"Because of your what?"
"*Sorek*."
"Ya lost me."
"*Sorek* was the valley where Samson fell in love with Delilah."
"Ooh, the temptress."
"Exactly."
"What?"
"The temptress."
"Ummm . . . ?"
"Samson would visit the valley of Sorek to see Delilah. He gave into temptation, and she tortured his secret out of him, lulled him to sleep, cut his hair, and called the Philistines to haul him off and put out his eyes."
"Like women, do ya?"
"What does that have to do with anything? You can't trust someone who'd sell you into slavery. I wonder if the last thing Samson saw was the woman he thought he loved mocking him."
"So it's saying to give you an easy road to follow, because otherwise you'll stray off to your guilty pleasure."

"Yes!"

"Okay, more."

Don't sell my soul to the oppressor,
For deceitful witnesses would have risen in me that puff out cruelty
Unless I had received the support of Yahweh on this earth.

Expect Yahweh.
Be resolute and let your heart be brave.
Expect Yahweh to act.

"So it's not just waiting."

"Nope. It's acting as if God's going to come through, even before He does. Parallel verse 14 to the second half of verse 6, and you can see that expectant waiting is honoring God when you've got nothing to give, singing and making music to celebrate His goodness."

"Crazy."

"Sure seems like it sometimes . . ."

"So when the world's trying to screw you over, you can be happy and live like it's all going to work out. Good luck with that."

"It doesn't say it's easy."

"But you're *supposed* to do it, right?"

"Not on my own."

"Yeah, yeah, I know. God helps ya."

"He better. I'm totally lost without Him. The psalms talk about consistently searching for God, asking Him tough questions, expecting Him to show up and change your circumstances, living like He's real, because He is."

"And you think that's gonna fix everything?"

"Maybe not make every problem disappear instantly. But don't you think things would start changing if people could look straight in the face of bullies and smile? If victims of violence stopped taking revenge? If we all started running to God for help instead of away from Him in fear? Expecting Him to show up and celebrating His love in the meantime?"

"Sounds good and all, but enough God talk. I'm hungry."

"Fine. Just don't forget that He wants better stuff for you than you do."

"Okay, fine! Now can we get some food already?"

"Sure. Where do you want to go?"

"Anywhere we want. Why should we be afraid?"

"You serious?"

"Nah, just thought I'd get your hopes up that I'm getting close to converting."

"Thanks."

Follow-up questions

1. How hard would it be to wait on God to rescue you if an army came charging in your direction?
2. In what specific ways do you seek God's presence on a day-to-day basis?
3. If Psalm 27 already talks about the ability of people to be in God's presence, why did Israel need a Savior?

On Your Side

Now if the most powerful Dude in the entire universe is on my
    side,
Who's gonna make me scared?
If His unbeatable, can't-be-stopped power is the ultra Duracell
    battery for this copper-top life,
Who's gonna make me afraid?
You can send your army of big, bad, gnarly and ugly lookin' rugby
    brutes
With their misshapen teeth all ready to eat my flesh and spit out
    my bones,
But all those enemies and foes are gonna fall flat on their collective
    face.
You can place politicians all around me,
Set up camp,
Start the most unjust war ever conceived and set it right on my lap,
And still I'm not gonna budge, won't quake an inch in fear,
'Cause He's here,
And I've asked Him to help me out,
And He likes me a lot,
So I don't have to beg or plead or wish He'll give me what I want
    on a lucky whim.
I've got free tickets to His house and I'm gonna use 'em,
Gonna be there every day and night 'cause He'll never refuse 'em.
They're good whenever I'm there.
It's the one thing I care about,
Getting a personal audience with the most beautiful lover of my
    soul.
When I'm in a hole, in a tight spot,
Not sure if I can get out or not,
He picks me up and hides me where I'm safe and warm.
He puts me up in the best digs without lettin' anyone do me
    harm.

So all those stupid Joes who wanted to drown me in their hate and
  lies
Are gonna have to look up at the sky to see just how high He's set
  me,
And that makes me so happy,
Gotta get it out with some dancin' and singin' and all around goofy
  white-boy floppin'
Like I got a learner's permit for tryin' to get down!

All over town you can hear me call,
Hear my voice, oh God, my King.
Don't let it zing past Your merciful attention.
Every time You've asked me to be like You that's what I've done.
And that's sayin' a lot
'Cause you know that sometimes before I've run away.
Please don't turn away from me.
Take pity on a man who doesn't have it altogether.
I'm Your servant.
Don't abandon me in my vulnerable moment.
My mom and dad could turn their backs, but You never will.
You welcome me every time I run to Your arms and show me how
  to live,
Give me smooth paths so my feet don't slip.
There's still all those ugly, flesh-chompin' dudes all around, so don't
  make it too difficult.
Don't let me succumb to their devious will.
I've heard their threats,
Their lies,
All the ways they want to mesmerize my heart with fear.
Every breath they breathe is a cruel and violent sneer.
I was near to giving up,
But You wouldn't let me quit.
And now I've got rock solid confidence that I'm gonna see Your
  face,

Not just in heaven, but here on earth.

You told me I'm worth it for You to go out of Your way to bless me
with presents I don't deserve,

Pour out rivers of goodness for everyone in the world

No matter who's in power, which country they live, or what they
believe.

You're so kind and gentle to all the damaged places in my heart.

It's makin' me start to feel better already just thinking about how
good You are to me,

No need to worry,

And I'm definitely not gonna be afraid.

After all, we've all got the One who planned, designed, and spoke
the entire universe into existence on *our* side.

Do You Dream Big Enough? – Psalm 72

Think about what Solomon knew a young king needed: wisdom, righteousness, and justice. He wrote this psalm (or it was written during his reign). He'd experienced his father's rule, and knew the prophecy God had given David about the coming One who would sit on the throne of Israel forever. Some of that prophecy applied to him. His own kingdom foreshadowed the real fulfillment that was too good to fully imagine. That's what you need to keep in mind to start understanding Psalm 72.

The psalm is written in groups of three. The first three parts mirror the second three parts, while the final, seventh part, is a mini-group of three reflecting God's character in the Messiah.

The fact that the psalm is in seven parts shows it reflects the creation story. It also reflects (as does the creation story) the seven-day temple dedication ceremonies that were common in the surrounding nations. Solomon himself took seven years to build the Temple, dedicated it in the seventh month, and had a celebration that lasted seven days. Then the Israelites extended the celebration for another seven days, because they were having such a good time.

These ceremonies prepared a building to be a god's home. On the seventh day the god (or God) was said to enter the temple and take his or her rest. Solomon's writing about the Messiah coming to physically live in His temple, the earth, which of course, is the fulfillment of all creation.

Here's a breakdown of Psalm 72's order:

1. (vv.1–4) Justice and righteousness for everyone, especially the poor and needy
2. (vv.5–7) Abundance in His kingdom and great prosperity for the righteous
3. (vv.8–11) All peoples serving Him and even His enemies bowing before Him
4. (vv.12–14) Salvation and exaltation to favored status for the poor and needy
5. (vv.15–16) His everlasting reign, prosperity, and abundance of His people
6. (v.17) The whole earth serving Him and being blessed through Him
7. (vv.18–20) Blessing God and fulfillment of David's prayers and God's promises.

Think about the coolness of all that. A king's going to come who will rescue the poor, the needy, the helpless, and all those who are oppressed. He'll give His people justice because He surrounds Himself with so much goodness that He can't make a mistake (that's the picture they had for righteousness). His justice makes sure that those who oppress others can never do it again.

He offers prosperity and so much peace to those He rescues that they forget how to be afraid. He says "they will fear you" and then follows it up with Himself coming down like showers of gentle rain, causing the righteous to flourish and fill the earth with beauty. Fear and reverence of Him spring from seeing His heart for goodness, not His power for destruction.

The mentions of the sun and moon don't just indicate that His reign will last a long time, although that's part of it. The sun and moon predicted the weather and foretold good or bad events to the ancient mind. So "abundance of peace, until the moon is no more" (NKJV) is a poetic way to say that peace will flood us continually, no matter what the omens say. They'll become obsolete in the Messiah's kingdom.

Verses 8–11 say that all kingdoms will bow down before Him. Even outlaws – "those who dwell in the wilderness" (NKJV) – will come submit to him, because He's the most merciful and just. Everyone who sides with evil will get their faces shoved in the dirt and never be able to hurt anyone again. Even the most exotic and powerful kings will present Him with honor ("offer gifts").

Verses 12–14 show His subjects serving Him because of the purity of His character ("His name"). Have you ever heard of a ruler who declared it His priority to rescue the needy? Then once He'd returned everything they lost He'd take the time to exalt them to nobility status in His kingdom ("precious will be their blood in His sight")? If you ever see that, it's God's heart. He loves it when we start to look like Him.

Verses 15–16 parallel verses 5–7. He's going to live forever and cause the earth to experience more abundance than we've dreamed possible. The most precious, exotic presents ("the gold of Sheba") on earth will belong to Him. It's going to be one huge party with food ("grain on the top of the mountains. Its fruit shall wave like Lebanon") and people living happily.

Solomon caps it off by saying that the Messiah's reign will be the greatest thing forever ("His name shall endure as long as the sun") and cover the earth. He'll share his glory with his people ("and men shall be blessed in Him"), and everyone in the world will love having Him as king ("Yes, all nations shall call Him blessed").

Verses 18–19 aren't just Solomon getting excited. He's saying, "God's character is exactly the same as the qualities He's assigned to the Messiah. He's already fulfilling these promises through my reign as king, and He'll bring even more completion to them when He comes to reign on the earth forever!" Look at His qualities: He does things better than we think He will, like justice for the poor and wiping out oppression. His character (His name) causes everything to flourish. He deserves to be revered and worshiped by the entire earth.

Then it says, "The prayers of David the son of Jesse are ended." That seemed weird when I first read it, and it seemed like a throwaway statement, but then I realized that David had gotten the original promise about Messiah coming through his line. So I think Solomon is saying, "This is the fulfillment of everything my father dreamed of. This is everything that God was saying to him. This is how it will be when his prayers come to pass."

It's not just the fulfillment of everything God promised David. It's the fulfillment of everything anyone's ever hoped or dreamed. Do you dare to hope for a God and a Savior that good? Yes! Do it God! May Your kingdom come, Messiah!

Follow-up questions

1. Why does this psalm give so much emphasis to the Messiah rescuing the poor and needy?
2. If the Messiah's kingdom took over your community, what else would happen beside the poor and needy getting rescued?
3. How are *you* the fulfillment of your parents' and grandparents' dreams?

We Don't Need Another Human Revolution

When a jury can't recover an abuse victim's innocence,
We don't need another human revolution.
When an overthrown tyrant sounds a prelude to more violence,
We don't need another human revolution.
When skin color still paints a sickening shade of ignorance,
We don't need another human revolution.
When money, fame, and power provide an excuse for greed and
    decadence,
We don't need another human revolution.

We need a Greater than we've been to recreate the earth,
Flood every square inch with justice,
The kind that stands the poor up to look the wealthy in the eye
    and smile,
People flock to the ghetto to live in harmony with style,
The red-light district becomes a playground for children,
Poverty ceases for all generations of the poor,
Oppressors lying broken in pieces forevermore.

When cynicism has replaced the patience of our hope,
We don't need another human revolution.
When the wedding of prince and commoner is just a daytime soap,
We don't need another human revolution.
When men don't see women as sisters anymore,
We don't need another human revolution.
When divorce splits love in a bitter tug-of-war,
We don't need another human revolution.

One day a beauty will rise,
Reflecting the radiance of the One who fills her eyes
With the light of His goodness, the rains of abundance.
All peoples, every nation, endless generations on earth

Will bask in so much peace
We won't need the moon to remind us of sunlight's dawn.
The earth yearns for peacemakers that conquer fear with song.

When children get sacrificed for the sake of adult convenience,
We don't need another human revolution.
When fathers turn to monsters who abuse in place of tenderness,
We don't need another human revolution.
When police beat an innocent man's skin instead of protecting it,
We don't need another human revolution.
When politicians can't remember what it's like to be a servant,
We don't need another human revolution.

Every kingdom and philosophy will bow at His gaze.
Even bandits and rebels find hope in His face.
Every Hitler, Inquisition, ethnic cleansing, superstition
Wiped clean, laid out flat, breaking evil's jealous back.
You can't stop His love attack. Don't even try to imagine that,
Because He fights for the weak,
Makes them more glorious than the sun,
Lives with more joy than anyone's seen.
He gives better than you've dreamed.

When a real Savior arrives and ends religious debate,
We won't need another human revolution.
When victims and oppressors forget what it means to hate,
We won't need another human revolution.
When our beauty's only surpassed by the radiance of His heart,
We won't need another human revolution.
When we welcome Him in, our real life starts,
We don't need another human revolution.
We need the Messiah.

God of the Nursing Home – Psalm 71

Fluorescent light streams cold through the halls. A man ten years younger than you pulls his wheelchair along the siderails. Just a couple more doors until you reach the one you want. You shuffle a few more steps, stop and turn. "B. Weston" the nameplate says. Brian hasn't been quite the same since he lost his foot, but it'll be good to see your old friend again.

"C'mon in. I'm decent."

"Brian?"

"Joe! Thanks for stoppin' by. When was it now, you last came?"

"Thursday. Last week . . ."

"Oh, right. Thursday . . ."

His memory might be foggy, but his half-cocked smile peeks through the wrinkles. It's good to see the old Brian light up in his eyes. Stories flow through your memories like the richest glasses of wine. After what seems like five minutes, it's been two hours. You have to go. A friendly hug and then it's back through the halls to the front door.

"See ya soon?"

"What's that, Brian?" You turn around outside his door.

"Come back soon, huh. It's been fun like . . . the last, uh . . . when did you last come again?"

"Last Thursday."

"Right. Thursday. Darn brain just don't work the same."

"Mine either. Don't worry. I'll be back soon."

Everyone seems friendly enough, but you can't imagine yourself here. The loss of freedom. The food. Still, who knows what could happen. Only three years ago, you and Brian spoke together at conferences and played a round of golf when you could fit it in.

As you close your car door, you remember the poem you wrote fifty years ago . . .

In you, Yahweh, I seek protection,
Don't let me be put to everlasting shame . . .

The problems you faced then live a world away. God stuck by you when it seemed like everyone else gave you up for dead. You've been leaning on His help ever since. Now your own mortality looms. Robert, your brother-in-law, seems to hatch a weekly scheme to harass your travel schedule. When you arrive home, you settle behind your old desk and grab a pen. The words pour out . . .

In You, Yahweh, I seek protection,
Don't let me be put to everlasting shame,

In Your justice, You'll snatch me up and help me escape.
Stretch Your ear to me and deliver me.

Be my safe house, where I always enter.
You've commanded me to be delivered because You're my hideout and fortress.

Snatch me out of the hands of criminals, my God,
Out of the hand of the unjust and cruel man.

For You're my lifeline, Master Yahweh, my trust since my youth.
I've leaned on You since my mother's womb. You're the one who cut the umbilical cord. My passionate songs forever sing of You.

Many consider me a miracle, but You're my strong shelter.
My mouth is full of Your passionate song and Your beauty all day.

Don't throw me away in my old age.
Don't abandon me when my strength is finished.

For my enemies have spoken at me.
Those who watch my soul have schemed in unity,

Saying, "God has abandoned him.
Chase and catch him for no one will snatch him away."

God, don't be far from me.
My God, hurry to my aid.

Let those who accuse my soul be put to shame and finished.
Wrap the ones who want my disaster in scorn and disgrace.

You stop writing in a bit of shock. The mortality thing must have weighed heavier on you than you thought. Your hands tremble slightly. Every emotion and hurt sits on your paper, in full view of God, and now you. When you perform it this will be the musical interlude, but for now you pick up your pen. You parallel the first verse, with a new perspective, the power of God beginning to surge through your fingers . . .

But I'll have continual confidence.
I'll increase my passionate songs to You.

My mouth will tell stories of Your justice all day long,
And salvations that are too many to count.

I will enter with the bravery of master Yahweh.
I'll remember only Your justice.

God, You've taught me since my youth,
And I still declare Your wonders.

And even in my old age and gray hair, God, don't You abandon me.
Until I declare Your power to this generation, Your bravery to all who will
come and your justice, God, to its full heights.

You, who have done so many, great things, who can compare with You?
You, who've let us, who've let me see so many tight spots and disasters,

You'll return to restore us, to restore me
You'll return to pull me out of the depths of the underworld.

You'll multiply my greatness
And surround me with Your comfort.

So I'll throw You thanks for Your faithfulness with guitar, God.
I'll sing my praise with a harp, Holy One of Israel.

My lips and my soul, which You ransomed, will shout for joy when I sing
my praise to You.
And my tongue will meditate on Your justice all through the day.

For the ones who want my disaster are ashamed.
They are humiliated.

In years past you might have danced to celebrate the victory you feel
inside. Now you bask, washing in the confident hope that lives in
your heart. You've watched God do so many amazing things. Why
wouldn't He keep it up?

"Do it for Brian, God. He may not remember everything, but Your
Spirit is stronger than his mind. Don't let him feel abandoned. Let
even his smile demonstrate Your power to everyone who sees him in
that nursing home."

Deep in your heart, you hear the tiniest whisper shout God's response: "Why would I value him any less than you?" Tears drip onto your writing. How could you ever deserve such love and connection from the King of the universe?

And God whispers even quieter, "How could I stop Myself from loving you?"

※　※　※

I kind of doubt that ancient Israel had nursing homes. But when I saw the same lines used for Psalm 71 and 31, one from an old man's perspective, it made me imagine the same writer writing them forty or fifty years apart.

Line up the first and second stanzas in Psalm 71 and see how each parallel verse contains common words. Notice the difference in attitude from one to the other. Look at what they say about who God is. Then go back and compare them to Psalm 31.

Whether you're young or old, God longs to surge His love through you. He can speak through any language, even the ones you forget. In Romans 8 Paul says that he's convinced that nothing can separate you from the love of God. If that's true, look forward to the days when your spirit shines so brightly, you won't need your words or mental faculties to communicate. Everyone will see the Father through you.

At some point your body won't have enough strength to contain your spirit. You'll need a better one that can handle all of God's awesome goodness. Then you'll finally be able to look at Him face to face.

Follow-up questions

1. What happens to someone's relationship with God when they begin to lose their memory?
2. When the idea of your own old age comes to mind, what do you think you'll be doing? Living at ease in retirement? Receiving the care of a nursing home? Something else?
3. What do you think heaven will be like?

Sunk in the Safety of God

I've sunk all my trust in who You are, God.
Don't let me fall in disgrace.
Your goodness must want to reach out and save,
Cause my soul to escape.
Open Your ears.
Whatever I fear, be the answer, my tower,
Shake the earth with power 'cause it's You I seek.
When the strong prey on the weak,
My life looks bleak,
Rescue me.
You radiate banners of hope through the growling storm.

From before I was born and all through my youth,
It was You that kept me safe,
So I sing what no man can take.
It's a miracle that I can stand unafraid,
But they don't know how strong You've made
Your tenderness deserves every epithet, exclamation, galaxy
    coronation of sun blazing goodness on Your crown.
When its rays sink down on gray hair, creaky limbs, a sagging body,
Don't leave me to the fangs of stronger wolves,
Hungry voices growling a pack of lies,
Sneering, "It's time.
No one will hear his screams.
God's abandoned his blood to our tongues!"

I need You to run,
Eyes furious, heart pounding.
Burn them up in Your anger.
Sweep away their plans.
Show the full strength of Your hand.
Shove justice into their bloodthirsty mouths.

Let the world hear of their shame, and Your rescue.
I've got newborn vision that only sees victory,
A tongue that's all dancin' glee, float like a butterfly, proclamating
    Muhammad Ali,
But it's not about me.
It's about the world seeing Your face, beaming,
Your feet running,
Invalids tasting wind on their lips,
Pleasures cascading from fingertips,
Lightning charging my heart,
Shooting through these words, because You deserve.
You deserve the submission and rejoicing of the whole earth.

O sweet and precious Friend, You've whispered the way for this
    boy to become Your man.
And that's why stories about Your miracles have to be told
From the old to the young, and future warriors to come.
Let this torch of good news run with leaps of joy until my final
    breath falls on Your heart.
Is there anyone so close, so full of mystery and life like You?
Through danger, terror, the abyss of doubt,
Not even hell could hold me out of Your grasp.
You don't just return me to the past, You make my future better,
    more glorious,
Pump Your groove degrees through the speakers.
I'm gonna sing celebrations of broken made whole,
Unload my soul's greatest treasure,
Bubble and spill joy into every day,
'Cause You're way too good,
And I'm still standing,
My feet planted firmly
In the safety of God.

The Best Magic Trick in the World – Psalm 19

Watch a magician. The next time you see Dynamo, Penn & Teller, or Jared Hall doing a trick, keep a close eye. They'll use their movements, their eyes, and their words to direct your focus where they want it. Outside your field of vision, the assistant escapes unharmed or the rabbit jumps into the box. And then they reveal something you never expected.

Look at Psalm 19. The writer's an illusionist. He uses parallel structure, and similar or contrasting statements, to lock your eyes on the imagery in each verse. He leads you on a tour of all creation and then all of God before arriving at a doorway you never see coming. I don't know if it's written by David, but the writer's good. Really good. It starts in the skies . . .

The heavens declare God's majesty.
The firmament displays what He's done.

When it says "heaven" it means the sky, sun, moon, and stars, everything you can see looking up. The "firmament" is a literal expression. Ancient Hebrew thought believed that a solid layer sat above the atmosphere. It opened and closed to allow rain, hail, and snow to fall.

You might think that it also separated the physical world from the realm of the divine, but you'd be wrong (tricked ya). The home of

God (or the gods) was considered a whole other dimension (cue the sparkly, mysterious music). To the ancients this says, "Look up! See how cool it all is? Notice how smoothly it functions and nourishes you. That's God at work. He's a master."

> Day after day they pour out messages.
> Night after night they communicate an intimate understanding.

Notice how the second verse connects to verse 1. "Pour out" fits with the Hebrew idea of the firmament. "Communicate an intimate understanding" fits with "declare God's majesty." It keeps the Creator front and center in your mind during the whole poem/song while the music grows richer.

> Their voice resounds to every language and dialect.
> Their message and order stretch to the ends of the earth.

> He made a home for the sun. Like a bridegroom bursting out of his preparation room with joy to run down the aisle.
> It springs from one horizon to the other. No one can escape its heat.

Two things I need to make clear before we go farther:

1) If you're trying to prove creationism or evolutionism through this psalm, you're a silly goof. That's not the author's point. He's using the imagery you experience on a daily basis to show you something about God's character. It's symbolic. It's art. It's beautiful. So is God. Stop looking at your own agenda!
2) You might not have noticed the similarity between a bridegroom running with joy and the sun blazing its heat. That's cool. I don't speak Hebrew either. But the smart people who do tell me that *Sammach*, the word translated as "rejoice," sounds a ton like *Chammah*, the word translated as "heat."

God's so cool He made the sun happy. And everyone in the world gets to enjoy it! That should tell you something about His heart. Let His warm yours to the same temperature, while the music stops swirling and becomes ordered and steady . . .

> The teachings of God are complete, refreshing the whole person.
> The evidence of God is unshakeable. It makes the naive wise.

Okay, this bit you *can* use when talking about the existence of God. You had the right idea, you were just a bit early and off on the creation stuff. The writer's saying, "We've seen God's work as a people. Huge miracles! We've tested what He teaches us. It works! We can tell you about it. It's pretty obvious that He's real and in charge. He'll refresh your soul if you let Him." See the focus? It's God wanting to point you to Himself, the source of all goodness. Make sure you don't pretend that it's telling you how He set it all up. Continuing . . .

> The principles of Yahweh are straight. They'll brighten your heart.
> The commands of Yahweh are pure. They'll make your eyes shine.
>
> The fear of Yahweh is completely clean and lasts forever.
> The justice of Yahweh is reliable, it's absolutely right.
>
> They're more desirable than gold, than a vault filled with the purest gold.
> They're sweeter than honey that drips fresh from the comb.
>
> Even more importantly, they warn your servant.
> And keeping them produces rewards.

Dang howdy, they warn ya. You get on the oppressor side of God's justice, and He's got a destruction button that could nuke the whole universe. I take Him seriously when He tells me to steer clear of danger . . . most of the time.

And talk about rewards, that part about honey dripping off the comb into your mouth is almost erotic. You follow God and He'll drop tasty morsels of pleasure in your tongue so pure, you might forget the joys of married love. No, not forget. The ecstasy will be enhanced! Cue the bow-chicka-bow-wah swanky guitar and saxophone . . .

Okay, continuing on (in chaste and holy purity) . . .

If you could sort out my mistakes, acquit me of hidden wrongs,
Even more importantly, keep me from arrogant actions and don't let them control me . . .

Hold it. I thought we were talking about the beauty of God's creation, His power, His goodness, His pleasure, His justice, His ability to change every part . . . of . . . me? Whoa. Me. I didn't see that coming. All of the earth rejoices to please God. All of God's words delight in doing His will. Does all of me? Does all of you?

God, could You keep me from the evil of my own selfishness?

. . . Then I'll be complete
And acquitted of all my wrongdoing.

May the words in my mouth, all the thoughts in my heart
Bring pleasure to Your face, Oh Yahweh, my fortress and the close relative who pays to get back my honor and inheritance.

I guess I could have just said, "my redeemer" at the end. But that doesn't tell you how good Yahweh is or what the writer actually wrote. He used the word that means "kinsman-redeemer" to describe the God of the universe. That was the person in your family that would say, "You're worth it. I'll take whatever debt you owe or disgrace you've earned all on my own reputation so you can be part of the family again."

God doesn't require you to be perfect before He accepts you. He may be clean and spotless and all powerful, but He comes to find you. He'll wade through the darkest dungeon, take on the scariest monster. He'll do whatever it takes to win your heart. He'll clean you up, give you a glorious destiny and call you His most precious daughter, His favorite son.

That's His promise. It's the best magic trick the world's ever seen, because it's no trick. He'll really go to the ends of the earth for you. Will you let Him?

Follow-up questions

1. What's the best magic trick you've ever seen in your life?
2. How many instances of God's intervention can you point to in your life that demonstrate how reliable He is?
3. If God truly will go through the filthiest, shame-filled swamp to make you part of the family again, what do you have to do to get Him to do that for you?

Creation, the Word, and My Heart

Starry hosts,
Sunset hues,
Tapestry of heaven,
Woven with fingers that caress baby skin,
Bend black holes to their will,
Whisper behind jagged mountain peaks, still desert scenes,
Singing gospel choir get-downs and Asian-stringed symphonies.
Skies swarm with melodies eager to worship.
Cymbals crash.
Waves rejoice.
The crown of sun splashes horizons with fire,
Blazes its golden trail,
Filling the earth with light,
Delighting to share its heat,
Reflecting God's perfect joy to mortal man.

Flawless laws,
Steadfast commands,
Holy decrees,
Purified truth and holy lips,
God speaks.
Our souls drip with warmth and love,
Wonder and awe,
Glorious splendor reborn,
Enlightened minds,
Sparkling eyes,
Carefree spirits,
Oh, to kiss His sweet voice forever,
No treasure too precious to trade,
No sacrifice too costly to surrender,
Every sentence blankets safety and peace,
Restoring life endlessly.

What man clothes himself like creation?
Whose thoughts radiate purely the Word of God?
Wash away all my secret flaws.
Don't let me impose my own laws.
Where no darkness hides,
A clean conscience skips free and light,
Radiating holiness to the world.

May every word I speak,
The deepest thoughts I think,
Bring an everlasting smile to Your face,
Author of all truth,
Singer of the starry hosts,
God who endures my shame to call me son.

The End . . . of This Journey

You've made it . . . through thirty, or actually thirty-one, of the psalms. Only 119 more to go. I hope you saw things you've never seen before. I pray that you've caught at least one glimpse of God's character that shot an overdose of love into your heart.

Writing this book has challenged my own perception of the King. It's been the most rewarding of all my writing. He's way better than I believed. He's also way more powerful. Don't get yourself on the side of His enemies. He's more merciful than anyone else, but He doesn't mess around with evil. He'll do whatever it takes to protect those who run to Him for protection, even if it means ending you.

I've seen so many people get caught up in the emotion and passion of worship. They say they'll do anything for God. They sing songs and act good for a while. And then they fade away, go back to the way they were before, or worse, or just disappear. Passion springs from commitment, not often the other way around.

If you didn't write out one creative thought while reading this, you're in danger. Go read the Bible, see if what I wrote is true, and dedicate some time each day to being with God. Once you close this book you'll have a million things demanding your attention. You'll be like the man that James talks about who only listens and never lifts a finger to do . . .

He is like a man observing his natural face in a mirror; for he observes himself, goes away, and immediately forgets what kind of man he was.

But he who looks into the perfect law of liberty and continues in it, and is not a forgetful hearer but a doer of the work, this one will be blessed in what he does. (Jas 1:23–5, NKJV).

You've got the freedom to live in the promises that Yahweh's made to you. Apply them to your life. Ask Him for His help. Tell someone else what you've discovered. You'll start growing in every season, like the man described in Psalm 1. No matter your emotions, you'll find a deep peace and the goodness of God enabling you to look whatever circumstances you face straight in the eye and say, "Bring it on!" The King of the universe has got my back.

See you soon,

Peter.

PS: A quick quiz

1. What does it mean that God will make your horn grow? Do you remember? If you don't, go back and find out. It appears in seven psalms that aren't in this book and two that are. I'm not going to explain it again. We've got other, cooler stuff to talk about next time.
2. What's a *tehillah*? Better find out . . .

Okay, last one, promise.

3. When you *zamar*, are you singing or playing an instrument? Can you remember? Think about it for a bit. No? Good. I didn't talk about it. But it's used in the psalms in this book. Go find out about it in a concordance and figure out which psalms from this book use it. Report to me for extra credit. Seriously. I'll send you something cool.

Now you've got homework. Add writing something for fun to it. Bye!

My Overly Long Thank Yous

On 17 September 2000 I was spending time with Jesus, reading Psalm 42, when the phrase, "Deep calls unto deep," (NKJV) burrowed its way through my heart. "I have to write this," I thought. Out came "Deep-sea Creature," the poem I included in the chapter on Psalm 42 about plunging so deep into the ocean of God's love that you have to be changed so you can live there. It still calls to me today.

A couple years later Psalm 36 caught my attention. "I don't think I appreciate the scope of what it's saying here," I thought. "I don't think most of the people who read it do. What if I wrote a stanza about each of these verses? They need to be felt. God's desire pulses with so much greater force than we can imagine. I have to write this."

Psalm 100 followed, then Psalm 27. Pretty soon Psalm 146 wore a tailored suit of modern language and pop culture references. I found myself not so much rewriting psalms, but attempting to communicate the same message from a completely different angle. I felt the freedom to use language and images not typically associated with religious conversations, as long as they stayed true to the God the psalms reveal. In fact, they kept piling the passion of my desire higher with licking flames of God's love.

Thank you, God. Thank you, Jesus. Thank you, Holy Spirit, for giving me the gift of Your Self. You didn't have to value me or create me. Nothing I do could hope to match Your beauty. Everything good I say about You is an understatement. You planted the seed for this book. You've watered it with people I don't deserve. You burn with the desire for this to grow into way more than any one-man performance. You long to pull the world to Your arms by showing us Your beauty. Thank you for being the Most Powerful Dude in the Universe and My Own Personal God. Thank you for being My Friend, Lover, Deliverer, Healer, Cheerleader, Mother, Father, Sister, Brother, ad infinitum . . . I'll never stop discovering You.

✳ ✳ ✳

"You should write the Spoken Groove Psalms," Steve Hawthorne told me in the Waymakers office as we worked together in the summer of 2005. "It would take a long time, but you know what would be better?"

"What?" I asked, nervously.

"Getting other people to engage with the psalms and write their own versions."

His eyes got wide like dinner plates. I couldn't escape his enthusiasm. I'm pretty sure about twenty pages of excited expository followed about how cool it was, but it was that phrase that never left me: "You should write the Spoken Groove Psalms."

Thank you, Steve, for believing in me and entrusting me with one of your pearls of vision. Those summers we worked together, prayed together, cried together, and encouraged each other become a more precious treasure to me every year. This book never would have happened without you showing me how to dive headfirst into the love of God. Prayer has become less of the discipline and more of the adventure and conversation that God always intended it to be because of you.

✳ ✳ ✳

In November 2009, despite having already penned five poems inspired by different psalms, I finally gave in to Steve's suggestion. I tackled

Psalm 45. I didn't write it as much as edit it a word at a time. It came out jagged and poking. I felt sure it would suck . . . until I read it. I don't know how it became magical and full of rhythm. It sure didn't flow out that way. It pushed me to continue, no matter how inspired I felt.

Five months later, Roy H. Williams, the Wizard of Ads himself, listened to me read a few of my poems from the psalms to him in his office. "These are good. You need to write the notes that go with them. People are going to want to know how you came up with some of these. Don't show me any more until you've got a finished product that you can sell. I'll be too tempted to tell you how to change them."

He was right. He usually is. I opened another file of notes, researching the psalms, searching for glimpses of the original psalmists' viewpoint of God. It took me longer, but I discovered deeper wells of refreshment. I couldn't believe the writing genius I discovered. God appeared far brighter, richer, and more terrifying than anything I'd dared to imagine. My project began invading my devotional time with God.

Thank you, Roy, for your generosity and commitment to my writing career. You told me of my potential before I understood the sacrifice it would cost. You found ways to keep me fed when finances ran low. You remained committed when I annoyed you to no end. I probably can't overvalue how far you've pushed me to fly.

❄   ❄   ❄

The next month I traveled to England to finish recording a CD and perform a couple shows. The first one came at the end of Andy and Emily Baker's wedding. I had no idea how a 45-minute spoken word performance would go down at a wedding reception. My eyes kept trying to shut from the jetlag of my flight. But Andy asked for everyone's attention, and they hushed. Strength from an unseen source filled me. That evening turned magical during "Love Complete," ending with a blessing and heartfelt prayer for their marriage.

"I'd love to help you in any way I can with your career," Andy said.

"You're not going to remember anything that happened tonight," I told him.

"I'll contact you when I get back from our honeymoon," he assured me.

Three weeks later he emailed me like he said. Not long after we agreed to work together. It hasn't always been fun, or even financially profitable. But Andy's always done what he said he would do.

Thank you for that, Andy. Faithful men like you are rare. I would never have completed this book without you believing that I had something worth supporting.

※　※　※

In May 2012, Andy introduced me and my newly-wed wife, Vicki, to Malcolm Down and Authentic Media. He's the first agent/publisher/label executive to seem eager to work with us. Most don't let me get past their email inbox. The rest send me away or run screaming when they discover how underground and description-defying my performance style is. Malcolm's eyes glowed with genuine friendship.

Thank you, Malcolm, and Authentic, for seeing more than a line on your ledger sheet in my eyes. Thank you for valuing the true beauty and talent of my wife. You have no idea how much that means to both of us. You accelerated the completion of this book and opened the door for something more than a book to bloom.

A special thanks needs to be said to Claire Musters, Becky Fawcett, and the rest of the Authentic staff who've challenged my writing and forced me to write a better book than I would have on my own. I don't know if you'll be mentioned somewhere else in the book, but you deserve lots of credit and respect for the work you do. I can't say thank you enough.

※　※　※

A couple months later Vicki and I visited the home of Yancy and Lynette Smith. They go to Christ Fellowship, the church in Fort Worth that allowed me to steal Vicki and bring her to Austin. Yancy's a Bible translator, pretty excellent scholar and great guy to talk to.

After talking about some of the things I was discovering in my psalms project, he said, "A little while ago I accidentally ordered two copies of this book. Now I know why." He walked to another room, returning with a book. "This guy's work is really thorough and he seems to be incredibly passionate about knowing God." As I read the title, *Ancient Near Eastern Thought and the Old Testament*, I had no idea how much it would aid my understanding of ancient Hebrew culture.

Thank you, Yancy, for valuing me as a peer, rather than some idiot who had no idea what he was talking about. Thank you, Lynette, for making us feel at home and lending your husband to me. You guys are so good at validating people and making them feel honored. At least, that's what you've done for Vicki and me.

❊   ❊   ❊

In January of 2013, as I struggled to finish, *Exposing the Psalms*, I met Mark Divine, former commander of Navy "SEAL" team 3. He attended my "No One Told Me How to Write Workshop" at Wizard Academy in Austin, Texas, and said that he wanted to be able to write his story better. In February, he emailed me with a chapter of the book he was co-writing with someone else. When I gave him my feedback, he asked if I would be able to improve another book he was writing.

I became his writing coach and editor, and helped him re-write *Eight Weeks to Seal Fit* in a month. Forcing him to write his true-life stories showed me what my research notes on the psalms needed to become.

I began a passionate descent into the abyss of God's love. He attacked my brain with more than I could handle. He flooded my eyes, pried open all my veins, and left me helpless to resist His goodness love syrup. I still can't describe the love affair that's raging.

Thank you, Mark, for trusting my instruction and advice, and for providing the spark that pushed me to the finish line. I know God better because of our friendship. I hope we remain friends forever.

❄   ❄   ❄

Once I finally submitted the "final" manuscript to be reviewed by Authentic, I began telling people about different chapters in it. I made the mistake of reading the chapter on Psalm 18 to Steve Laswell, a business coach who had just become one of my marketing clients.

"Love to share your Psalm 18 story/chapter/piece with Rita and re-read . . . on one knee . . . any chance?" he wrote me in an email the next day.

A few weeks later I finally read it to both of them as they drove to Oklahoma City the day before Easter. Steve began asking me open-ended questions about how I'd written it. A long conversation ensued. Then he asked me if I'd thought about ending each chapter with some open-ended questions to get people to think about and investigate each psalm further. Once again I knew it needed to be done.

Thank you, Steve, for being more than a client. Thank you for challenging me to be a leader who cares more about the journey of others than my own. Thank you for listening and for asking.

❄   ❄   ❄

The one person who's heard more about this book than anyone other than God is Victoria. She's my bride, my sexy lover, and best friend. I've coerced her to "listen to this story" or "check this out" or "tell me what you think about this" so many times. She watches me weep as I get overcome with how good God is. I thought she'd grow weary of me long ago. She loves me more. She improves my writing, makes me explain things more clearly and more powerfully.

She creates space for me to create and creates art of her own in everything she does.

I don't deserve you. Thank you, my darling, my sweetheart, for loving just me. I love how our honeymoon keeps getting sweeter with each passing moment.

❋   ❋   ❋

Long before I thought of writing this book, I watched my brother's eyes sparkle with passion as he talked about worship, the presence of God, ancient Hebrew worship and the psalms. He's twenty-one months older than me, and we've been close, both in proximity and relationship, for nearly all our lives. Most people get the impression that I desperately long to show him up or beat him at everything. They're probably mostly right.

Secretly, you're my hero, Dave. I never would have pursued God as hard, never would have embraced the discipline of excellence, never would have learned to listen to and enjoy people without experiencing your brilliance. Thank you for fighting to keep our relationship close. Thank you for provoking my curiosity to explore mysteries. I'm glad I don't have to repay you.

❋   ❋   ❋

Dad, you've given me a glimpse of how the Father loves and forgives. Your creativity makes me wonder how you're possible. Your faithfulness is a lighthouse in the midst of every storm. I hope I grow up to be half the man you are.

❋   ❋   ❋

Mom, God's tenderness has always rushed through your arms and words to my heart. You radiate more of God's beauty than you've ever noticed in the mirror. Thank you for training me in the way I should go. Thank you for bathing me in prayer. Thank you for reminding me that I'm born in Zion.

❊   ❊   ❊

To the rest of my family, Lisa, Mark, Kayla, Sam, Janna, Ethan, Anne, Schoichi, Brian, Matt, Steven, Amy, Rosemarie, Beck, Haddie, Joe Sr., Donna, Joe, Gina, Bob, Grace, Hope, and Micaiah, thank you for calling me one of your own. You represent far more blessings than I will ever deserve. I hope we always grow closer together and never gather merely from obligation.

❊   ❊   ❊

To Olen and Sybill Griffing, Robert Morris, Rocky and Margaret Gathright, Bill Leckie, Elias Reyes, Jim Morton, Wayne and Bonnie Wilkes, Alan and Yvette Latta, Brian Johnson, Steve LeBlanc, Mary and Bill Burns, Lamar and Cindi Howell, Ron and Janine Parrish, Mark and Susan Buckner, Britt and Jonelle Tucker, Sean and Shannon Jones, Ryan and Erin Walker, Clark and Natalie Zaunbrecher, Declan and Diane Fleming, Clyde and Kitty Howell, Dave and Dea Bresemann, Jim and Cynthia Brannon, Amy Padgett, Andy and Sarah Combs, Zach Ball, Julie Ogan, and Tom and Pam Ball. Thank you for caring for my soul. I know so many who carry wounds and scars from pastors and spiritual leaders. I beam with gratitude and long to know God more because of your example.

❊   ❊   ❊

To Mark Oestreicher and Sarah Etheredge, thank you for listening to the recommendation to book someone you'd never heard of for Youth Specialties and Soul Survivor (respectively). Your openness to my art has changed the course of thousands upon thousands (perhaps millions!) of lives for good. May God bless you crazy big.

❋ ❋ ❋

To all the friends around the world who have booked me to perform at their church, school, club, restaurant, festival, business, home, or "other" venue, opened their home and gave me a warm place to sleep, cooked me food, paid for my dinner, bought a CD, T-shirt, DVD, or book, signed up for my email list, said something encouraging, gave me a hug, or smiled, thank you! Books need to be written about how cool each one of you is.

❋ ❋ ❋

Finally, thank you for spending your time (and maybe your money) to read this book. No one accomplishes anything alone. May you receive far more than you've given.

Thank you,
Peter Nevland.

Bibliography

Bulkeley, Tim, "Evidence of Idolatry and Polytheism in Ancient Israel", 1996–2005, http://bible.gen.nz/amos/culture/polyth.htm (accessed 2010–13).

Gill, John, *John Gill's Exposition of the Bible* http://www.biblestudy-tools.com/commentaries/gills-exposition-of-the-bible/ (accessed 2010–13).

Henry, Matthew, *Matthew Henry Commentary on the Whole Bible* http://www.biblestudytools.com/commentaries/matthew-henry-complete/ (accessed 2010–13).

Hensley, William Ernest, 'Invictus' Poetry Foundation (2013) http://www.poetryfoundation.org/poem/182194 (accessed 7 October 2013).

http://ancient-hebrew.org/12_wayofyahweh.html (accessed March 2013).

http://ancient-hebrew.org/33_shofar.html (accessed March 2013).

http://ancient-hebrew.org/emagazine/010.rtf (accessed March 2013).

http://ancient-hebrew.org/emagazine/045.rtf (accessed March 2013).

http://ancient-hebrew.org/emagazine/055.html (accessed March 2013.)

http://buddysheets.tripod.com/hebrewwordsforpraise.htm (accessed March 2013).

http://ehow.com/list_7496332_ancient-way-refining-silver.html (accessed March 2013).

http://en.wikipedia.org/wiki/Zion (accessed March 2013).

http://gotquestions.org/sons-of-Korah.html (accessed March 2013).

http://hispresentglory.net/glory2/index2.php?option=com_ content&do_pdf=1&id=49 (accessed March 2013, site since removed from the internet).

Israel Weather, "Climate Information for Mount Hermon and the Mount Hermon Ski Resort," http://israelweather.co.il/english/ week.asp?tbSelCity=6.

Jamieson, Robert, Fausset, A.R., and Brown, David, *Commentary Critical and Explanatory on the Whole Bible* (1871) http://www. biblestudytools.com/commentaries/jamieson-fausset-brown/ (accessed 2010–13).

King James Version Bible (1769) http://biblestudytools.com/kjv/ (accessed 2010–13).

Knowles, Melody D., *Centrality Practiced: Jerusalem in the Religious Practice of Yehud & the Diaspora of the Persian Period*, (Atlanta: The Society of Biblical Literature, 2006).

Mazar, Amihai, *Archaeology of the Land of the Bible 10,000–586 B.C.E.*, (The Anchor Bible Reference Library, New York: Doubleday, 1992).

New American Standard Bible (La Habra, California: The Lockman Foundation, 1995).

The Holy Bible: New International Version (Colorado Springs, CO: Biblica, 1984) http://www.biblestudytools.com/niv/ (accessed 2010–13).

New King James Version Bible (Thomas Nelson Publishers, 1975) http://www.biblestudytools.com/nkjv/ (accessed 2010–13).

New Living Translation Bible (Wheaton, IL: Tyndale House Publishers, 1996) http://www.biblestudytools.com/nlt/ (accessed 2010–13).

Segal, Rabbi Benjamin J, "(Hearing and) Seeing is Believing", *A New Psalm: a new look at age old wisdom* (15 June 2010) http://psalms. schechter.edu/2010/06/psalm-17-hearing-and-seeing-is.html and http://psalms.schechter.edu/2010/12/psalm-42-3-why-so-down-cast-my-soul-text.html (accessed 15 June 2013).

Bibliography

Sendrey, Alfred, *David's Harp: The Story of Music in Biblical Times* (New York: The New American Library of World Literature, 1964).

Stern, Ephraim, *Archaeology of the Land of the Bible, Volume II: The Assyrian, Babylonian and Persian Periods (732–332 B.C.E.)*, (The Anchor Bible Reference Library, New York: Doubleday, 2001).

Strong's Concordance (2013) http://www.biblestudytools.com/concordances/strongs-exhaustive-concordance/ (accessed 2010–13).

The Message Bible (Colorado Springs: NavPress, 2002) http://www.biblestudytools.com/msg/ (accessed 2010–13).

Walton, John H., *Ancient Near Eastern Thought and the Old Testament: Introducing the Conceptual World of the Hebrew Bible* (Grand Rapids, Michigan: Baker Academic, 2006).

Young's Literal Translation Bible (2013) http://www.biblestudytools.com/ylt/ (accessed 2010–13).

Authentic

We trust you enjoyed reading this book
from Authentic Media. If you want to be
informed regarding the next publication in the
Tree of Psalms series
and other exciting releases you can sign up
to the Authentic newsletter online:

w.w.w.authenticmedia.co.uk

Contact us:

By Post:
Authentic Media
52 Presley Way
Crownhill
Milton Keynes
MK8 0ES

E-mail:
info@authenticmedia.co.uk

Follow us: